North by Northwest

Director
Alfred Hitchcock

Note by Dan Williams

Longman   York Press

York Press
322 Old Brompton Road, London SW5 9JH

Pearson Education Limited
Edinburgh Gate, Harlow, Essex CM20 2JE, United Kingdom
Associated companies, branches and representatives throughout
the world

© Librairie du Liban *Publishers* and Pearson Education Limited 2000

All rights reserved. No part of this publication may be reproduced, stored in a retrieval system, or
transmitted in any form or by any means, electronic, mechanical, photocopying, recording, or
otherwise, without either the prior written permission of the Publishers or a licence permitting
restricted copying in the United Kingdom issued by the Copyright Licensing Agency Ltd,
90 Tottenham Court Road, London W1P 9HE

First published 2001

ISBN 0-582-45253-8

Designed by Vicki Pacey
Phototypeset by Land & Unwin (Data Sciences) Northampton
Printed in Malaysia, KVP

contents

background 5
trailer	5	■ cary grant	14
reading north by		■ eva marie saint	15
northwest	6	■ james mason	15
key players' biographies	10	■ bernard herrmann	16
■ alfred hitchcock	10	■ saul bass	16
■ ernest lehman	13	director as auteur	17

narrative & form 22
narrative structure	22	space and time	33
characterisation	26	equilibrium and	
themes	31	disequilibrium	34

style 37
mise-en-scène, camerawork		editing	42
& framing	37	■ the crop-dusting scene	44
■ lighting	40	sound effects	48

contexts 51
ideology	51	■ VistaVision	60
■ gender	54	■ filmography	61
film contexts	57	other cultural contexts	66
■ the industry	57	critical responses	68
■ production history	58	the audience	71

bibliography 75
cinematic terms 79
credits 81

author of this note Dan Williams teaches Film Studies for the department of Continuing Education at City University and is a visiting lecturer in Film and Television Studies at Brunel University. He has also written the York Film Note for *Citizen Kane* (published 2000).

background

trailer *p5*   reading North by Northwest *p6*
key players' biographies *p10*   director as auteur *p17*

trailer

Metro's *North by Northwest* is the Alfred Hitchcock mixture as before – suspense, intrigue, comedy, humour. Seldom has the concoction been served up so delectably. It should be top box office.

Variety, 1 July 1959

In all this is a luxury product which cannot fail to appeal to all kinds of audience and to provide them with spy-thrill entertainment at its very best by a master of the genre.

Daily Cinema, 4 September 1959

... the film as a whole is a grand item of entertainment which alternately will have the audience on the edge of the seat or enjoying a hearty laugh.

Motion Picture Herald, 4 July 1959

The reviews of *North by Northwest* when it was released in 1959 show that the film was appreciated for its entertainment value. The film also succeeded with audiences and by the end of 1959 it was the sixth most popular film of the year at the US box office. In this study we will examine how skilful storytelling and expression through film form are responsible for the entertaining qualities of *North by Northwest*. We will consider in detail how narrative and the film's style convey meaning. We will also examine a number of contexts that offer greater understanding of *North by Northwest* and critical debates that relate to the film.

reading

background

a problem of mistaken identity

reading north by northwest

The central idea of the story is that a man is forced to flee from villains who seek to kill him due to a problem of mistaken identity and from the police because he is mistakenly identified as a murderer. The story is told in a way that draws on the conventions of **classical Hollywood** cinema. The main character, Thornhill, is established as a New York advertising executive involved in his work and preoccupied by arranging a visit to the theatre with his mother. The opening **scenes** allow the film to emphasise the central role of Cary Grant, one of Hollywood's most successful stars at the time, as the character of Thornhill. Within minutes the story involves a dramatic, shocking twist as Thornhill is abducted by sinister thugs. Tension is created around the question of how Thornhill will survive and a sense of mystery prevails about the reasons for the abduction. The chief villain, Vandamm, persists in his belief that Thornhill is an adversary named Kaplan. Since Thornhill refuses to cooperate, he is condemned to death.

One reason why the film is so entertaining is its combination of different **genres** The suspense and shock developed around Thornhill's abduction are typical effects of the mystery thriller. However, Thornhill's response to this dangerous situation contains elements of comedy. The film draws on Grant's established skills as a comedy actor, and includes witty ironic dialogue. The opening is so successful partly because comedy and suspense are interwoven, seeking to keep the viewer alert, and suggesting that the film will be full of shocks and surprises. The sudden disruption of Thornhill's daily life encourages curiosity about how the story will develop.

The rest of the film draws on other genres. Vandamm's role as a character who is seeking to trade in government secrets introduces the significance of espionage in the story. The emphasis on mystery and crime is combined with the spy thriller in which a hero has to combat enemies of national security. Thornhill's escape from Vandamm's men and the refusal of the legal authorities to believe his story mean that he is propelled on a

background   reading

a romantic male icon

journey. Events compel Thornhill to cross America from New York to Chicago, to the plains of South Dakota and ultimately to the monument of Mount Rushmore. Thus the film draws on the adventure genre as the hero is forced into various spectacular situations of danger.

Thornhill's journey can be described as **picaresque** since he appears to be led on a meandering course in which the point of destination changes in response to events created by other characters. The journey has an overall pattern in that it is influenced by the conflict between Vandamm and the American security services. This is a conflict in which Thornhill appears to be an innocent victim. The journey also has a pattern because Thornhill follows approximately a northwest direction. The title of the film plays on this. It also refers to an airline named Northwest, which is shown when, near the climax of his journey, Thornhill arrives at an airport.

Finally, the film involves romance. Fleeing from Vandamm's men and the police, Thornhill meets Eve Kendall. The narrative suddenly changes here to emphasise the flirtation and attraction between these two characters. Eve Kendall is played by Eva Marie Saint, who had won an Oscar for best supporting actress in On the Waterfront (Elia Kazan, 1954). She was twenty years younger than Grant when North by Northwest was made and less established as a star. It is clear that the meeting between these two characters draws on Grant's reputation as a romantic male icon who could be immediately attractive to a younger woman. Since Hollywood film narratives so frequently include romance, we may question whether it should be regarded as a genre. Nevertheless the film displays a recurring quality of Hollywood romances – an emphasis on delaying the point at which love is realised.

The mixing of romance with other genres ensures that the happy union of Thornhill and Eve is withheld until the penultimate shot of the film. Their relationship is presented in a way that emphasises the confusion created by mistaken identity. Here there is a reversal of the initial situation in which Thornhill's identity is confused with that of Kaplan. When Thornhill falls for Eve he does not realise that she is a secret agent. The espionage thriller context complicates the romantic plot, resulting in Eve's role undergoing two significant changes. At first she is Thornhill's saviour,

reading background

a treacherous femme fatale

providing refuge from the police. Then she is presented as a treacherous femme fatale who plays a role in arranging the attempt to assassinate Thornhill on the prairie. By the end of the film she is redeemed, setting up the finale where she becomes Thornhill's wife.

It can be argued that the dominant genre in the film is the thriller: the narrative is clearly sustained by continuous twists in which our understanding of the situation faced by Thornhill suddenly shifts. However, given the emphasis in the second half of the film on the relationship between Eve and Thornhill, romance appears to hold an equal status within the narrative.

In *North by Northwest* the central idea of an innocent man on the run is developed in a way that makes us believe that Thornhill will survive. This confidence comes partly because of the film's comic tone, including Thornhill's humorous remarks at points of danger. Also, the use of an established star in this role means that an audience is unlikely to expect Thornhill's early removal from the narrative. Hitchcock's reputation for creating suspense and Hollywood's emphasis on pleasing a mass audience mean that audiences for the film could reasonably assume the hero would survive. For a more detailed analysis of the **theme** of the innocent man on the run, see Narrative & Form: Themes and Style.

Close analysis of how the narrative is organised and the approach to film form and style will provide a deeper understanding of how the film succeeds as entertainment. We will look at the contribution made by the pace of the narrative and the use of spectacular action scenes, and consider how far the film relies on conventions such as a cause and effect pattern in the narrative and **continuity editing**. These conventions, like the use of genres and stars, are found throughout classical Hollywood cinema.

North by Northwest has been celebrated not simply as successful popular entertainment – it has been argued that it should be accorded a higher cultural status (see, for example, Bordwell and Thompson, *Film Art*). The recognition of *North by Northwest* as an original work of art was developed by critics concentrating on Alfred Hitchcock as a director with a distinctive style. When looking at the creativity behind the film we also need to examine the role of others involved in the production, including the

background reading

significant red herrings

screenwriter Ernest Lehman. The collaboration between Lehman and Hitchcock in developing ideas for the story and Lehman's declared aim to write the 'ultimate Hitchcock film' suggest that while the director's career is central to the ideas behind the film, the contribution of others, such as Lehman, should also be fully recognised.

In the narrative of *North by Northwest*, we can observe the use of a typical Hitchcockian device, the 'MacGuffin' – a narrative device that, as Hitchcock explained, appears central, but ultimately proves insubstantial to the conclusion of the story. In *North by Northwest* the belief that George Kaplan exists leads to the dramatic event of Thornhill's abduction. The search for Kaplan also provides a basis for Thornhill's actions as he seeks to act independently of the police. And yet, as the film reveals in the first scene involving the secret service, George Kaplan does not exist. He is a decoy set up to fool Vandamm and distract attention from the work of Eve as a double agent. It could be argued that the invention of Kaplan fits with Hitchcock's recurrent reliance on a MacGuffin.

The film also includes other significant red herrings. Discussing the film in the interview with François Truffaut (see Bibliography), Hitchcock makes it clear that the MacGuffin is actually the way in which events are propelled by factors that ultimately have no significance within the story. In *North by Northwest* the struggle between Vandamm and the counter-espionage agency is about government secrets, but the nature and significance of these secrets never becomes an issue. This is why Hitchcock claimed that in *North by Northwest* 'the MacGuffin has been boiled down to its purest expression: nothing at all' (Truffaut, 1966 p. 195). The film reveals that Vandamm's actions involve trying to smuggle secret government information on a microfilm, which is ultimately shown to be hidden within an African statuette. Despite the importance of this information, which leads both Vandamm and the security services to act ruthlessly to defeat one another, the contents of the microfilm are never revealed. The microfilm provides a source of motivation within the narrative but it remains significant as an object whose real value is defined only in general terms.

The use of devices that resemble Hitchcock's notion of the MacGuffin provides an indication of the originality of *North by Northwest* as a

reading background

the contrast between silence and sound

Hitchcock film. Although some critics have regarded the film as one of his best, there is debate as to how it compares with his other films. Is *North by Northwest* weaker than *Vertigo* (1958), for example, because the former appears to be more light-hearted? How does *North by Northwest* compare with Hitchcock's films made in Britain? Some argue that his work in America represents a stronger artistic achievement, freed from limitations imposed by the British film industry. Through close analysis of the form and style of *North by Northwest*, we can reach a more informed position from which to assess what makes Hitchcock's work original and how this film compares or contrasts with his others.

key players' biographies
ALFRED HITCHCOCK

When analysing *North by Northwest* it is relevant to consider Hitchcock's emergence as a film-maker during the silent era as well as his subsequent career. The crop-dusting scene, in which Thornhill is attacked by gunfire from an aeroplane, depends upon creative use of the contrast between silence and sound. Hitchcock directed films during the 1920s in Britain that already displayed a distinctive approach. For instance, his control over editing and camerawork is responsible for the particular approach to suspense in early films such as *The Lodger* (1926). With *Blackmail* (1929) he responded in a very creative way to the introduction of sound. While many British films from this period have been criticised for relying on a style which is similar to theatre, Hitchcock extensively explored the distinctive possibilities of cinema as a medium. He took a strong interest in film styles developed in other countries, including the **montage** editing of Russian film-makers and expressionism developed in German cinema (see Other Cultural Contexts).

Although films directed by Hitchcock remain closest to the dominant style of classical cinema, it is striking that throughout his work aspects of film style are used to create the sense of an 'authorial presence' within the film (Bordwell, Staiger and Thompson, 1985, p. 79). Hitchcock's brief appearance in his films comically illustrates this strategy. In *North by Northwest* he is

background — biographies

inventive approach to film style

seen in the opening sequence just missing a bus, an event that humorously foreshadows a moment in the crop-dusting scene when Thornhill is left alone after a bus departs.

Hitchcock's films make extensive use of the convention of **point of view shots**, often concentrating on the visual perspective of an individual character, whilst also including sudden switches to more unusual camera angles. It has been argued that when these changes in the style of the film occur the audience becomes more aware of Hitchcock's direction. Even in his use of point of view shots Hitchcock showed originality early in his career, revealing events sometimes from a position that was exactly that of the character looking (known as optical point of view) rather than a position which is just to the side of the character looking, the convention used by many directors (Bordwell, Staiger and Thompson, 1985, p. 79).

Although Hitchcock has been critically respected for his inventive approach to film style, it is important to recognise that from the beginning of his career as a director he absorbed effects achieved by other films. Born in 1899 in Leytonstone, just four years after the first film had been publicly screened in Paris, Hitchcock grew up as the new culture of cinema expanded and developed throughout the world. Donald Spoto in his biography of the director, *The Dark Side of Genius - The Life of Alfred Hitchcock*, draws attention to the fact that Hitchcock's childhood involved the quite different experiences of education in a strict Catholic school and exposure to the new, sometimes sensational offerings from early films that he saw as a child. Some of the moments of exhilarating action in *North by Northwest*, such as Thornhill standing in the middle of the road as a huge lorry heads straight towards him, can be compared with the appeal of early trick films that depicted dramatic collisions and accidents.

How far biographical information about Hitchcock's personal life can explain the nature of his films is a matter of debate. Spoto draws attention to aspects of Hitchcock's upbringing and character that can be related to the films, discussing, for instance, an anecdote Hitchcock told about his childhood. According to the director, his father punished him for something when he was six by sending him to a police station with 'a note'. The officer responded by locking the boy in jail for five minutes (Spoto,

biographies   background

lifelong exploration of fear

1994, pp. 16-17). This incident, alongside Hitchcock's other anecdotes about fear experienced as a child may, as Spoto suggests, provide an explanation for Hitchcock's lifelong exploration of fear as a cinematic subject. Spoto also discusses Hitchcock's particularly close emotional relationship with his mother (Hitchcock was fifteen when his father died), and his relative detachment from other pupils at school. According to Spoto, throughout his life Hitchcock had an interest in 'practical jokes' and 'macabre' subjects, and displayed specific traits such as a desire for total control over his work. Recent research on Hitchcock's working methods by Dan Aulier, however, also reveals that the director allowed members of his production team considerable freedom in their contribution on films such as *Vertigo* and *North by Northwest*.

In 1925 Hitchcock married Alma, a screenwriter working in the British film industry. Later in his career he made *Mr and Mrs Smith* (1941), a film that alluded to his marriage proposal to Alma on a voyage at sea (Spoto, 1994, p. 238). Perhaps the initial flirtation between Eve and Thornhill on a train reflects Hitchcock's personal interest in romance developed during a journey. The Hitchcocks were married throughout his life, with Alma helping him on a number of productions.

Hitchcock's single-minded concentration on a particular area is evident in his film-making right from the beginning of his career: throughout his working life he consistently worked in the thriller **genre**. *North by Northwest* also provides a striking example of Hitchcock's exploration of variations on a theme. This film invites obvious comparisons with other work such as *The 39 Steps* released in 1935 (see Contexts: Filmography). However, Hitchcock was also continuously innovative. It could be argued that *North by Northwest* is more conventional than some of his other films. It certainly provides a contrast with the film that followed, namely *Psycho* (1960), which took the thriller genre into new shocking territory. Nevertheless, with *North by Northwest* Hitchcock came close to controversy, choosing to shoot the final sequence against the setting of Mount Rushmore, a national monument that displays huge carvings in the cliff-face, represcnting the faces of four American presidents.

Film historians have discussed how Hitchcock's work changed with his

background — biographies

the sly mix of terror and teasing humour

move to America in 1938. He was attracted by the creative opportunities that Hollywood could offer. After Hitchcock's international successes in the mid 1930s with films such as *The 39 Steps*, the producer David O. Selznick signed him and collaborated with him for the next ten years. *North by Northwest* emerges at a point when Hitchcock had been working with a relatively settled production team for a number of different studios. From the start of his career in America Hitchcock moved between studios, due initially to arrangements made by Selznick. There were periods when he made a series of films for an individual studio, such as his work for Paramount in the 1950s, but in comparison with other directors he achieved a position of considerable independence. When Hitchcock's own production company failed in the early 1950s he continued to work on a semi-independent basis. *North by Northwest*, despite its success, was a one-off project for the studio, Metro-Goldwyn-Mayer. Hitchcock developed a style of directing that involved very thorough planning before the production, so that editing of the film and post-production work were kept to a minimum.

ERNEST LEHMAN

Born in New York in 1920, Lehman studied Creative Writing at college, moving on to become a copy editor for the *Wall Street Financial Journal*, and a publicity writer for Hollywood (see Kemp in Jeromski (ed.), pp. 489–90).

Lehman wrote a wide range of **screenplays** during his Hollywood career but *North by Northwest* was the only one not adapted from a pre-existing text. Four of Lehman's screenplays were adaptions from broadway musicals: *The King and I* (1956), *West Side Story* (1961), *The Sound of Music* (1965) and *Hello Dolly* (1969). One of Lehman's other successful screenplays, *The Sweet Smell of Success* (1957) was adapted from his own novella, but Lehman had to leave the production of this film before it was completed.

He wrote one other screenplay for Hitchcock, the director's final film – *Family Plot* (1976). The screenplay for *North by Northwest* has been widely praised. For example, it has been said that this screenplay 'deftly captures the sly mix of terror and teasing humour that typifies Hitchcock's cinema

biographies — background

'a perfect dreamboat'

at its best' (Kemp in Jeromski (ed.), 1997, pp. 489-490). Lehman had some difficulties in writing the screenplay but Hitchcock encouraged him to continue, helping to put aside worries about what was required by MGM.

CARY GRANT

Originally named Alexander Archibald Leach, Cary Grant was born in Bristol, England, in 1904. At the age of thirteen he ran away from school, joining a group of performers and acrobats and subsequently travelled with them to New York. Grant became very successful as a comedy star in the 1930s.

Hitchcock resisted the proposal by MGM to use their stars – Gregory Peck and Cyd Charisse – for *North by Northwest*. Hitchcock had worked with Grant on three films previously – *Suspicion* (1941), *Notorious* (1946) and *To Catch a Thief* (1955). *North by Northwest* provided an opportunity to present a variation on this previous work. Hitchcock's conviction that Grant was the right actor for the part of Thornhill may also have been based on Grant's earlier success in screwball comedies of the 1930s and later hits such as *The Philadelphia Story* (1940).

In screwball comedies during the earlier part of Grant's career, such as *His Girl Friday* (1940) and *Bringing Up Baby* (1938), ridiculous circumstances force the Grant character to adapt and improvise while misunderstandings proliferate. Grant's character in these films is not the epitome of a strong male hero, but rather that of a man who has to cope with zany circumstances and strong-willed female characters. At the same time, he is not completely undermined, thanks to his charisma and his ability to participate in a fast-talking world of comic banter and absurdity. The Thornhill character displays a variation on this capacity for survival, although the film's thriller narrative means that the obstacles he encounters are quite different.

Despite Grant's success as a comic actor throughout the period of the Hollywood studio system, he had also established status as a romantic male lead. As Steven Cohan points out, Grant has been described as 'a perfect dreamboat' (Schickel, quoted in Cohan, 1992, Screen v33 n4, p. 407). Grant was hugely popular and successful. He has also been called 'an authentic American hero' (Rothman, quoted in Cohan, p. 394) and 'a national

background — biographies

an image of 'eternal youthfulness'

monument' (Cavell, quoted in Cohan, p. 394) despite the fact that some of his roles suggested a bachelor character with irresponsible tendencies. In the role of Thornhill, Grant is at one level obviously middle-aged (grey-haired and twice divorced) while he is also shown as being youthfully energetic and attractive to a younger woman. This indicates Grant's success at maintaining an image of 'eternal youthfulness' (Cohan, p. 395).

Grant's image was so popular that he had been the first major star in the Hollywood studio system to achieve independence, and during the fifties had considerable control over which films he appeared in. During the production of *North by Northwest* he became anxious about the part and had to be persuaded that the film would succeed. Looking closely at Grant's techniques, James Naremore points out that the actor had established a reputation for conveying very precise expressions, a skill put to good use as Thornhill responds to a series of incredible circumstances (Naremore, 1988, pp. 213–35).

EVA MARIE SAINT

Eva Marie Saint was born in New Wark, New Jersey in 1924. She received an Academy Award for her first film role in Elia Kazan's *On the Waterfront* (1954). She played a character who appears to be vulnerable but is strong inside (see Kaminsky, updated by Salamie in Unterburger (ed.) pp. 1077–8). Hitchcock plays against this image, making Eve Kendall tough and cool in the way she deals with the world, but lacking the strength to see through Vandamm without the professor's assistance. Despite critical praise for her performance in *On the Waterfront*, Eva Marie Saint's career included few other cinema roles. She appears in *Exodus* (Otto Preminger, 1960) and *Grand Prix* (John Frankenheimer, 1966).

JAMES MASON

Born in Huddersfield, England, in 1909, James Mason became a star of British cinema in the 1930s and 1940s. He was particularly successful playing the part of romantic villains – for instance he is the highwayman in *The Wicked Lady* (Leslie Arliss, 1945). After acclaim for his role in *Odd Man Out* (Carol Reed, 1947) he moved on to Hollywood films including his performance in *A Star is Born* (George Cukor, 1954).

biographies

conveying suspense and tension through music

BERNARD HERRMANN

Herrmann first worked with Hitchcock in 1954, composing the music for *The Trouble with Harry*. His subsequent work for the director included the music in *Vertigo* (1958) and *Psycho* (1960). Before working with Hitchcock, Herrmann had established his reputation as a film composer with work that included the music in *Citizen Kane* (1941).

The soundtrack for *North by Northwest* shows Herrmann's skill at conveying suspense and tension through music. It has also been observed that the score captures the spirit of the film being 'exuberant' and 'witty' (Milicia in Jeromski (ed.), 1997, pp. 376-9). It brings to the fore a series of elements in the story including humour and romance, but also reflects the pace of the story. Herrmann used 'seventh chords', and a 'particular choice of melodic fragments, harmonies and orchestrations combined make his work very distinctive' (Milicia, in Jeromski (ed.), 1997 p. 379).

SAUL BASS

The striking design for the opening credits was provided by Saul Bass, who also worked on *Psycho* and *Vertigo*. Before his career in film production Bass was a designer of film posters. His work on film openings has been critically acclaimed for its aesthetic qualities. With *North by Northwest* the diagonal lines of an abstract pattern initially provide the backgound for the credits, including the distinctive lettering of the title. The grid-like pattern of the lines materialises into the image of an imposing skyscraper with the blurred reflection of traffic and passers-by in the street. Distortion provided by the blurring hints at the disorientation that will be explored in the film. The change from the initial abstract pattern is also made more dramatic by the transition in colour from an abstract green to the **'realistic'** colours of the reflected street scene. The latter sets up the opening sequence set in the bustling centre of Manhattan as the credits continue until the point where Hitchcock makes a cameo appearance.

background — **director as auteur**

director as auteur

We have already noted aspects of narrative and film style cultivated by Hitchcock's direction – narratives that use a 'MacGuffin', produce suspense and surprise, involve striking use of unusual camera angles and sometimes include optical **point of view shots**. We will now consider in more detail the idea of Hitchcock as an **auteur** and then note alternative views on how we might approach this idea of authorship.

The concept of the auteur was developed initially by film critics working for the French film journal *Cahiers du cinéma* in the late 1940s and 1950s. They discussed the work of certain directors as art on the basis of original style. Hitchcock was one such director given the status of auteur on the basis of a distinctive approach to film-making. Writing about Hitchcock in 1958, Eric Rohmer and Claude Chabrol discuss the director's work up to this date, and their analysis combines appreciation of Hitchcock's style with discussion of thematic ideas in the films. In particular they argue that while Hitchcock worked in the thriller genre he consistently explored the idea of 'transference of guilt' whereby an apparently innocent character becomes involved in a situation in which they cannot be morally pure because they are affected by the guilt of another character.

Hitchcock's films address psychological issues in a way that arguably draws on his Catholic background, prompting a need for confession and redemption before a narrative is concluded, or these films may leave the audience with a degree of ambivalence as essentially good characters struggle, at the level of psychology as well as action, with the problems of a dangerous world. In *North by Northwest* Thornhill finally has to face his conscience when he is told that Eve Kendall is a double agent whose life has been endangered by his actions. Eve is also shown struggling with inner conflict when she is forced to act for the villain Vandamm against Thornhill. Emphasis on the moral transformation of Thornhill is central to an analysis of the film by Robin Wood. William Rothman's reading suggests that Hitchcock's direction in *North by Northwest* develops a confessional, cathartic quality towards the end of the film. These critical responses have informed the account of narrative and film form that follows

director as auteur — background

effects that may be called poetic

and will be examined more fully later (see Contexts: Critical Responses and Filmography).

A wide range of critics, including Wood and Rothman, have explored Hitchcock's films, drawing on the concept of authorship. It has been argued that another consistent theme in Hitchcock's films is the idea that a world of chaos and danger lies just below the surface of ordinary life, threatening to engulf characters at any point. In *North by Northwest* Thornhill is plunged into a life-threatening situation due to an accident as he is mistaken for the fictitious Kaplan. He is later pursued by the police as he is wrongly thought to have killed Townsend, the UN official whose identity had initially been assumed by Vandamm.

Auteurist analysis of Hitchcock's cinema has not always stressed moral themes. His films have also been studied in a way that places emphasis on aesthetic qualities alongside the exploration of psychological issues. Close attention to narrative and film form in Hitchcock's work reveals effects that may be called poetic. The way in which parts of *North by Northwest* deliberately echo earlier films by the director illustrates how a reading of the film can become more complex. We may be made aware of how variations in film form and narrative can be applied to similar subjects.

Hitchcock's approach to film-making is illuminated by his own discussion of the work. In an interview in 1967 Hitchcock suggests that his films use 'realistic photography' to make strange events more vivid for the viewer, and that his films seek to provide the viewer with the kind of extreme involvement associated with a nightmare. His comments also indicate that the viewer will ultimately recognise a lack of reality in the film. When the narrative concludes, the viewer will be relieved just as he or she would be happy to wake from a nightmare. Hitchcock said: 'The audience responds in proportion to how realistic you make it. One of the reasons for this type of photography is to get it looking so natural that the audience gets involved and believes, for the time being, what's going on up there on the screen' (Hitchcock, 1967, Interview with Herb A. Lightman, in Gottlieb (ed.), pp. 313–14).

Hitchcock's views changed during his career, but the idea of temporarily leading the audience into a state of nightmare has some relevance to

background   director as auteur

the audience is led wherever the director wishes

North by Northwest as Thornhill becomes attacked by both police and criminals. The film certainly seeks to transport the viewer into a different state of mind, which can be associated with dream or nightmares. Perhaps, however, this film contains more emphasis on the artificiality of the situation than, for example, *Psycho*.

Hitchcock's views on cinema authorship are also apparent in an article he wrote on the art of film for *The Encyclopaedia Britannica* in which he declares that: 'In the cinema the audience is led wherever the director wishes'. He believes that this power depends on the director's choice of images: 'The impact of the image is of the first importance in a medium that directs the concentration of the eye so that it cannot stray' (Hitchcock, 1965, Gottlieb (ed.), 1997, p. 216). This emphasis on the image reminds us that Hitchcock's first experiences as a film director occurred in the silent era. It is clear that he perceives a decisive difference in the roles of director and screenwriter. It is also interesting that Hitchcock stresses the role of film editing in a way that suggests that it sets cinema apart from other art forms: 'To me, pure film, pure cinema is pieces of film assembled. Any individual piece is nothing. But a combination of them creates an idea' (Hitchcock, 1963, Cinema 1 no 5, in Gottlieb (ed.), 1997, p. 288).

One problem with concentrating on the director as an auteur is that we may underestimate how his or her approach is influenced by the work of other film-makers (see Other Cultural Contexts). We need to strike a balance between respecting Hitchcock's skill and seeing his work in context. As already suggested, it is also important to recognise the creative role of others such as Ernest Lehman in the development of *North by Northwest*. Since the emergence of the auteur theory, film studies has involved a range of other critical approaches. These include consideration of the way a particular film deploys conventions of narrative and film form. In the section on Narrative & Form we will look at individual examples that demonstrate both originality and conformity to the style of Hollywood film-making.

The auteur theory has also been criticised because the creativity of the director seems to be given more attention than critical discussion of values conveyed by the work. For example, Hitchcock's films frequently

director as auteur background

voyeurism and narcissism

involve characters who may be considered stereotypical. It can be argued that his films reinforce dominant ideas in our society. Another criticism of auteur theory is that our reading of the film should not just be a search for the personal expression of the director. Equal attention may be given to the role of other creators of the film, and we can bring our own values to the film. This may involve a critical reading of the film or expressing how it affects us as individuals (see The Audience).

A strongly critical approach to Hitchcock's work has developed drawing on psychoanalysis. Laura Mulvey (in Braudy and Cohen, 1985) argues that Hitchcock's films involve the viewer in voyeurism and narcissism. Voyeurism refers to the activity of looking unseen for sexual pleasure, or excitement. In psychoanalytical approaches to cinema the concept is used to describe a psychic response in the viewer elicited by film form and narrative. Since cinema places the viewer in the position of unseen observer, Mulvey's argument is relevant to a wide range of films. Indeed, Mulvey argues that Hollywood cinema in general tends to involve the viewer in this kind of response, but Hitchcock's *Rear Window* (1954) and *Vertigo* (1958) are cited as examples in which the reliance on voyeurism is more explicit.

These films do not involve explicit sexual images but the main female protagonist is presented in a way that emphasises her desirability to the male character. Through our **identification** with this character, developed by the narrative and camerawork, the female character is also established in a way that makes her glamorous appearance a source of visual pleasure for the spectator. Mulvey considers how the female character is presented as passive in many Hollywood narratives, at least by the end of the film. Shots from the point of view of the male protagonist are more dominant within the story and build up a sense of the control that he achieves by the end of the film due to the outcome of the story.

Narcissism refers to obsessive identification with an ideal image of oneself. Again, cinema in general presents the potential for this response as we identify with heroic figures. Frequently shots that represent a general perspective on the action are combined with a dominance of shots representing the male protagonist's point of view, encouraging identification with his situation. The responses of voyeurism and narcissism can be

background | **director as auteur**

a strong emphasis on Thornhill's point of view

related to *North by Northwest* where there is a strong emphasis on Thornhill's point of view and the narrative involves him in observing the actions of Eve at a critical point in the narrative. Even though Thornhill's ultimate struggle is with Vandamm and his men, his decision to spy on Eve is presented as a very important turning point in the struggle for power.

Mulvey's analysis and subsequent discussion of psychoanalytical issues in relation to Hitchcock's films is explored in greater depth than this summary can cover. The approach has led to debate since many critics do not accept that concepts such as voyeurism and narcissism can accurately describe our involvement as viewers in the film. These concepts may underestimate the extent to which the viewer remains aware through the film that the story is detached from his or her personality. Also, the narrative clearly affects our identification with the protagonist – for example, what is the extent of our identification with Thornhill as a character, given that the first half of the film puts such emphasis on his position as a victim? Nevertheless, the example of a psychoanalytical approach illustrates how discussion of the film can move beyond auteurist analysis to debate about how films influence the audience. For further discussion of the film's representation of gender, and how it relates to ideology, see Ideology; ideas relating to the audience will be developed in The Audience.

narrative & form

narrative structure *p22*   **characterisation** *p26*   **themes** *p31*
space and time *p33*   **equilibrium and disequilibrium** *p34*

narrative structure

David Bordwell has shown how classical narratives involve causes that are 'character centred' (Bordwell, Staiger and Thompson 1985, p. 13). In *North by Northwest* each character has aims that are maintained through the story, providing a sense of continuity. Following his abduction, Thornhill is motivated by his desire to investigate the mysterious figure of George Kaplan. He then seeks to confront Vandamm. After the murder at the UN, which he is falsely suspected of because of a preposterous situation in which he is left holding the knife, Thornhill's fight for survival becomes more intense, with the police and Vandamm in pursuit. Vandamm and his henchmen are motivated by their desire to thwart Thornhill, whom they mistake for George Kaplan. Vandamm is convinced that Thornhill is a secret agent who threatens the plan to smuggle secret government documents. The professor is motivated by the desire to investigate and combat the actions of Vandamm as an enemy of national security. This produces the scheme of creating Kaplan as a decoy and employing Eve as a double agent. Eve is motivated by her dedication to the cause of the security services but also becomes romantically involved with Thornhill.

The romance between Thornhill and Eve complicates the character motivations resulting from the espionage plot. The structure of cause and effect evident in clear-cut character motivation is also complicated right from the beginning by the advent of chance as Thornhill is accidentally mistaken for Kaplan.

Each action of the plot is carefully related to the actions that follow. For instance, in the opening sequence Thornhill gets up to send a telegram because he wishes to speak with his mother about their visit to the theatre. This in turn results from the fact that he forgot that his mother

narrative & form narrative structure

at key points information will be held back

was playing bridge and thus cannot be contacted at home by Thornhill's secretary as he instructed. The fact that Thornhill has to send a telegram because he briefly forgot the whereabouts of his mother shows how, alongside purposeful motivation, a character's mishaps or failings may act as a cause within the narrative.

The structure that dominates Hollywood film-making is that of the story based on character action and motivation. A clear pattern of cause and effect ensures that the film brings a level of comprehensibility to the audience. This approach to narrative also recognises the pleasure offered when one scene flows seamlessly into the next. Having said this, *North by Northwest* is very entertaining because it creates mystery. At the start of the film we do not understand why certain events occur. Nevertheless the tradition of classical narrative is maintained because the film reveals at a later stage the cause of actions which seem mysterious when they first appear. This organisation of the cause and effect structure is most typical of the crime or mystery genres, but other **genres** within **classical Hollywood** and popular cinema will involve holding back some crucial information that explains events in the narrative. *North by Northwest* involves then a mixture of two approaches to cause and effect. On the one hand the narrative is given a momentum showing events and actions that logically follow one another in a closely related chain, including the chase structure as Thornhill attempts to escape from Vandamm's henchmen and the police. On the other hand, at key points information will be held back to create curiosity, which is satisfied later as the causes are revealed.

The way cause and effect are organised within the story means that the viewer is faced with questions, but these are subsequently answered. (An approach to narrative that considers the structure provided by questions and answers can be found in Carroll, 1988, pp. 170-81.) Enigmatic or mysterious events are shown, but then they are on the whole satisfactorily explained. The viewer is engaged with situations in which the outcome is temporarily uncertain but is ultimately resolved.

Initially the most dramatic questions are raised by Thornhill's kidnapping. Why has this event taken place? Who has Thornhill been kidnapped by? What is the motivation of the kidnappers? Like the audience, Thornhill is

narrative structure narrative & form

atmosphere of mystery

also in a position where he lacks answers to these questions. As the car in which he is imprisoned enters the grounds of a country mansion we see from Thornhill's point of view a sign indicating that the resident is called Townsend. The illuminated sign and the grand approach to the house contribute to the sense of mystery, especially since Thornhill is held hostage by a couple of henchmen. In fact the sign is deceptive. We learn that Vandamm has taken over Lester Townsend's house only later in the story. A scene of revelation occurs midway through the film when the intelligence authorities are shown discussing Thornhill's situation. By this stage he has escaped from Vandamm's men twice and is wanted for the murder of Lester Townsend at the United Nations.

Significantly, Thornhill finds out about the causes of his abduction later than the audience. The variation between knowledge held by Thornhill and knowledge possessed by the audience allows a greater range of responses to his predicament. Initially we may identify with his astonishment at the abduction and his confusion over the identity of Townsend. Later we may view his actions from a more detached perspective because of the information revealed in the scene with the intelligence authorities, but also suspense is created because we know that they are not planning to save Thornhill.

The decision to reveal the cause of Thornhill's abduction after the UN murder means that the film is quite different from a 'whodunnit' style of narrative in which the answer to a central question in the story is usually withheld until the climax. *North by Northwest* becomes more explicitly a thriller since the villain and his motivation are identified at this stage of the story. An element of mystery is, however, maintained since further explanation of Vandamm's actions is not given until the point when Thornhill meets the professor.

Going back to the initial dramatic questions surrounding Thornhill's abduction, it is important to recognise that there is a balance between information provided and the atmosphere of mystery. Thornhill's first confrontation with Vandamm reveals that the latter is involved in a struggle with a rival organisation. It is clearly suggested at this stage that Vandamm is immersed in a conflict relating to espionage. It is, though,

narrative & form   narrative structure

the identity of an elusive figure

quite unlikely that we can anticipate that Kaplan is a fictional decoy invented by the intelligence service.

It is interesting that prominent questions raised by the narrative refer to identities. The question of Kaplan's identity provides Thornhill with a personal quest and allows Hitchcock and Lehman to generate fascination with the identity of an elusive figure. As Hitchcock revealed later, this idea of a fictional decoy came from a journalist at a dinner party who was happy to allow it to be used. In his recent research on Hitchcock, Dan Aulier includes copies of two letters from the journalist with suggestions for the story that ultimately became *North by Northwest*. These involved one or two key ideas and in no way detract from the skilful, creative development by Lehman and Hitchcock of the story.

Vandamm's assumption of Townsend's identity becomes apparent only following the murder at the UN. Nevertheless, a sense of enigma surrounding Vandamm's character develops right from the beginning as Thornhill places himself in the role of private investigator. One of his main clues is the photograph of Vandamm found in the hotel room, which provides a useful link in the narrative when Thornhill meets the real Mr Townsend.

As this account of the narrative suggests, the simple reliance on cause and effect allows a wide range of complications to take centre stage. Crime films frequently involve emphasis on the pleasure of such complications. In considering the narrative structure it is worth noting that certain questions within the story are left unanswered for a long period, whilst others are resolved quickly. Throughout the narrative we are confronted with the question of how Thornhill will survive. But this is broken down into more specific questions about how he can survive particular situations. For instance: how will he survive driving in an intoxicated state? How will he escape when the villains track him down again at the hotel?

Another question that receives a delayed answer concerns the identity of the double agent first referred to in the scene with the intelligence service. This question is not as startling as the question about Kaplan's identity. When the professor refers to his double agent, this simply seems to frustrate the sense that Thornhill could be rescued. The existence of the double agent is offered as a reason why the authorities will not intervene

narrative structure   narrative & form

an articulate, witty advertising executive

in Thornhill's situation. Later, however, the revelation that Eve is the double agent provides a major twist. We may anticipate this revelation, but the narrative scrupulously withholds the information until a point just before the climactic scenes at Mount Rushmore. Since this information is withheld, Eve's initial appearance is made more enigmatic – an apparently uncanny intervention, which keeps us guessing about her character.

characterisation

THORNHILL

Roger O. Thornhill is an articulate, witty advertising executive. At the beginning of the film we see him with his secretary, advising her to 'eat more', and noting that he must 'think thin'. He also asks his secretary to make the necessary call to arrange his theatre trip that evening with his mother.. This conversation takes place as Thornhill and his secretary move through the crowded streets of Manhattan, a location that serves to introduce him as an ordinary member of metropolitan, commercial life, while his slightly ironic words signify a man of distinctive humour.

The initiative he uses to acquire a taxi involves a streak of quick thinking, a character **trait** that later pays dividends in dangerous situations. We might also consider that he is portrayed with negative characteristics during the opening – shallow, superficial, dominating the conversation with his secretary and opportunistic in acquiring the taxi. One interpretation of the film is that it shows how this advertising man is shaken from his self-indulgent lifestyle but recovers to become a hero.

When Thornhill becomes the innocent victim of a bizarre kidnapping, his first reactions are disbelief and indignation, as well as some physical resistance. As Thornhill is forced into the kidnappers' car he continues to talk about what is happening as if it is a kind of practical joke. Thornhill's refusal to break down during the abduction establishes his capacity for heroic resistance. For much of the film his lack of fear is remarkable, allowing the light-hearted and comic treatment of grave situations. Thornhill's dialogue with the villains is actually more like a monologue since no one will believe what he says: his claims of innocence are

narrative & form — characterisation

just an ordinary citizen

interspersed with jokey remarks that are consistent with his identity as a sociable man who finds it easy to look at events from an ironic perspective. However, some shots indicate his sense of panic and his recognition of the threat posed to his life. Thornhill principally does not pause to reflect but acts swiftly in response to the situations in which he becomes embroiled. He is then a fantasy figure marginally connected to realist patterns of behaviour.

The light-hearted element in the presentation of Thornhill's struggle is maintained in part by his relationship to his mother, whom he even contacts when fleeing the police, wanted for murder. We never see Thornhill at home, but his conversations with his mother indicate that in some respects he is just an ordinary citizen involved in an amusing family relationship, which contrasts with the cold war situation that intervenes in his life. But the relationship with his mother is also stereotypical. She is briefly portrayed as slightly foolish, while Thornhill acts absurdly. It has been argued persuasively by Susan Smith that at one point we share Mrs Thornhill's amusement at the actions of her son (Smith, 2000, p. 56). In the lift scene when Thornhill's mother starts laughing at her son's claim that two strangers are there to murder him, the whole crowd in the lift joins in the laughter. Although we know that he is right, the scene presents a strange comic effect.

To an extent Thornhill's patterns of speech reflect his profession. As an advertising man he is able to come up with one-liners that catch our attention whatever the situation. The economy of his one-liners matches the need for speedy action and clearly draws on the use of humorous dialogue in the **genre** of screwball comedy. In his exchanges with Eve, Thornhill is quite extrovert. The dialogue between Eve and Thornhill in the scenes of sexual flirtation may seem crude at certain points but the brevity of the dialogue prevents the sexual aspect of Thornhill's character from becoming a dominant feature of the story. The sexual nature of the relationship between Thornhill and Eve is instead developed through the emphasis on ambiguity and changes in her character. Hitchcock famously stated: 'Suspense ... is like a woman. The more left to the imagination, the more the excitement' (quoted by Spoto, 1994, p. 398).

characterisation   narrative & form

a match for Thornhill

EVE

When they meet on the train Eve is a match for Thornhill, responding to his conversation with knowingness and irony. Vandamm also pretended to an intimate knowledge of Thornhill on their first meeting, but Eve goes much further, playfully flirting, matching Thornhill's need to evade immediate honesty with her composed directness.

She is a match for Thornhill in terms of social etiquette, taken to the point of absurdity as they casually discuss the menu, despite the constraints of the situation. She continues to act decisively and pragmatically. Like Thornhill she is a performer who adapts to her role with ease and sophistication, but as the narrative develops she shows, in moments of weakness, her hidden emotions.

So, an important issue is whether the film's representation of gender is misogynistic and reprehensible. A key point to consider here is the way Eve is depicted as contradictory. She appears to play a role in organising the attempt to remove Thornhill by the crop-dusting plane, but then she is moved to discover that he has survived and attempts to save him from further danger by ending the relationship. The audience is not definitely informed whether Eve knew that Vandamm was seeking to kill Thornhill. She may have felt that he could survive or may have thought that the plan to send Thornhill to the prairie was just a way of discouraging him from further involvement in a dangerous situation. However, the most obvious understanding is that she allowed him to be assassinated.

Thornhill wins Eve only through his persistence. His determination to investigate Eve's activities leads ultimately to a breakdown of her role as femme fatale. When it is revealed that she is a double agent we are encouraged to forget her acquiescence in the plan that could have led to Thornhill's death. It can be argued that through the character of Eve the film combines the fantasy of the femme fatale with the fantasy of the morally pure woman. We temporarily experience her as a cold, treacherous deceiver, but then she is saved by our understanding of how she is forced to act in a certain way because of her duties as a double agent. The viewer is allowed to decide how far Eve's early actions constitute a charade. By leaving her role slightly open-ended the film makes her transition

narrative & form — characterisation

an archetypal villain

from spy to Mrs Thornhill more ambiguous. The economy imposed on characterisation by the spy genre means that emotion and authentic character intentions are not developed as major issues.

To summarise: two serious problems raised by the representation of the main woman are firstly the problem of finding coherence in her character; and secondly the lack of depth developed in her character due to her mission as a spy. The woman of mystery perpetuates a stereotype found across a wide range of crime films. While Thornhill's light-hearted character is also a fantasy figure, he is given more scope through comedy and action to convey heroic qualities of resourcefulness, quick thinking and physical power (see Ideology: Gender).

VANDAMM

Vandamm is presented as an archetypal villain: cunning, ruthless and mysterious. We learn just before the final climactic scenes that he is, as the professor puts it, 'a kind of importer-exporter'. When Thornhill replies by asking what Vandamm is trading, the professor replies quite vaguely that it may be government secrets. The emphasis of the film is more on Vandamm's determination to eliminate Thornhill, once the latter has refused to cooperate, than on the specific nature of Vandamm's subversive activities. In a way, Vandamm's power is awesome, as demonstrated by his acquisition of Townsend's house, by his ability to have Thornhill followed by Eve, and then by the highly elaborate assassination attack using the crop-duster plane.

In the first meeting between Vandamm and Thornhill the film plays on certain similarities between the two characters. Vandamm is handsome, articulate and often speaks in an ironic way. The meeting suggests a confrontation of equals. Vandamm feels that he is up against his main adversary. He tries to show that he can see through Thornhill's pretences. Ultimately, however, Vandamm's ironic banter shows that he is mistaken about Thornhill. Later the rivalry between them is developed in their competition for Eve.

Vandamm operates by delegating responsibilities to Leonard. Vandamm's masterful position outside the action cultivates the mystery around his

characterisation *narrative & form*

a man of culture

character. He is represented as a man of culture. Eve refers to her initial impression of Vandamm's charm. His first appearance in a grand house introduces the idea of a man of style. Later his appearance at the art auction reaffirms the association with high culture. At the end, Vandamm's house near Mount Rushmore conveys sophistication with the modernistic style of the celebrated architect Frank Lloyd Wright. However, these associations do not really reveal Vandamm's character fully since his main aim is to operate outside the law, employing elaborate means to disguise his subversive actions. At the art auction he acquires the African statuette, but it is revealed later that this object is used to hide secret information on a microfilm. Vandamm's stylish apartment is a departure point, serviced with a private airstrip.

A more personal side to Vandamm's character emerges when he shows his feelings for Eve. He responds with anger when Leonard reveals that Eve is a double agent. Vandamm is too emotionally involved with Eve initially to appreciate Leonard's vital information and strikes his chief accomplice. The film plays comically on Vandamm's weakness of character at this point.

LEONARD

Leonard plays a vital role in the action but is developed even less as a character than Vandamm. Leonard is described in the screenplay as 'slightly effeminate'. He is stereotypically presented through a small range of character traits, keenly observing events around him and efficiently loyal to the cause of his boss.

THE PROFESSOR

The professor is another character who is presented in a minimal way. The film emphasises his calm, cerebral leadership of the intelligence authorities. He has the final word as this group discuss Thornhill's predicament. When the situation becomes complicated by the possibility that Eve's role as double agent will be jeopardised by Thornhill's actions, the professor intervenes personally. He is shown to be ruthless in acting to save his agent rather than out of concern for Thornhill. The professor's dedication to the national cause allows him to be quite manipulative in persuading Thornhill to help divert attention from Miss Kendall. The professor justifies

narrative & form

themes

an innocent man on the run

his actions with a speech about the realities of war. Ultimately he contributes to a happy outcome, arranging for last-minute assistance when Thornhill and Eve are just about to be vanquished by Leonard.

themes

The main **themes** are set up in relation to the character of Roger Thornhill. To start with, the theme of an innocent man on the run is developed as he is chased by Vandamm's men and by the police. This situation allows the portrayal of states of anxiety and the creation of suspense. Although the intelligence authorities are not represented in an explicitly sinister way their ineffectual position in relation to Thornhill's safety is maintained until the final stages of the film.

In conjunction with the theme of Thornhill's innocence, *North by Northwest* emphasises the protagonist's isolation. The story has an absurdist quality partly because we might feel at any point that Thornhill's best route to safety would be to insist more strongly that the police listen. Having decided that the authorities will not believe him, Thornhill decides that he must find Kaplan. The Gothic theme of Kaplan as a double of Thornhill is at least suggested while Kaplan remains so elusive. Like a supernatural double, or a psychological double haunting the hero, Kaplan fails to materialise. As the narrative develops, however, we become aware that Kaplan is simply an illusion used by the intelligence service.

Thornhill's quest to find Kaplan may hint at the psychological theme of a character who is fascinated by his own double. However, the film instead focuses on suspense and comedy in Thornhill's quest for survival. Right from the start Thornhill knows that Kaplan is different from himself. These differences are played for comedy when Thornhill investigates Kaplan's room, finding out that this mysterious stranger has dandruff and a smaller suit size.

For a number of critics the film carries a moral theme in the form of Thornhill's transition from being a selfish, shallow character to a heroic one (for instance, see the brief summary of Robin Wood's analysis of the film in Critical Responses). It could be argued that he behaves in a way

themes — narrative & form

the creation of illusions

that is self-centred as he pursues an independent investigation into the mysterious character of George Kaplan, dragging his mother along. As commentators on the film have noted, Thornhill's initials, R.O.T., inscribed on the match-holder that he shows to Eve, suggest, albeit in a light-hearted way, his lack of true heroic status. The way Thornhill falls for Eve also suggests a character who acts on immediate desires. Thornhill makes an important transition when he decides to act for Eve Kendall at the end.

However, an emphasis on his moral transformation appears to underplay the consistency in his character. Throughout he is a man forced to react to incredible circumstances: a man whose actions are frequently reactions and thus not necessarily that revealing of a change in character. Thornhill's journey through a series of dangerous situations calls for reinvention which can be regarded as part of the theme of love. Romance is shown developing in the context of danger. Thornhill discovers a new wife only accidentally, because his mundane daily existence is shattered.

The theme of theatrical manipulation and illusion is evident in *North by Northwest* as a whole. Although we may not recognise this theme at the start, it is introduced with Thornhill's intention to visit the theatre with his mother. The abduction intervenes to replace this plan with a world where appearances are deceptive. Since no one will believe Thornhill, he is forced to make up his own lies and carry out a kind of improvised performance. Throughout, Thornhill adapts to situations of danger despite losing an easygoing, apparently secure world. Vandamm's efforts to maintain secrecy around his activities are like elaborate theatrical illusions, including, for example, the acquisition of Lester Townsend's house. The dialogue from Vandamm and Leonard refers to a world in which false identities are an integral part of the work by the intelligence services. Leonard refers sarcastically to the skill with which the authorities can convincingly conceal the true identity of their agents. Later, in the auction scene, Vandamm is contemptuous of Thornhill's apparent role-playing, emphasising the confusion resulting from role-play.

The creation of illusions is made into a vital element in outwitting the opposition. The shooting of Thornhill by Eve involves both characters acting out a scene of personal conflict before the elaborate stunt of

narrative & form — space and time

spectacular action and surprising juxtapositions

Thornhill collapsing to the floor, with the professor as a supporting member of the cast who acts as a concerned member of the crowd.

The historical context of the Cold War affected some Hollywood films of the 1950s, leading to representations of sinister figures seeking to infiltrate and undermine American society. *North by Northwest* keeps this scenario as a context rather than developing an explicit message about international conflict (see Contexts: Ideology). Nevertheless, the context of a political struggle of grave significance determines how we understand the characters' actions. For instance, Eve's commitment to her work as a double agent is finally represented as dedication to a national cause. Thornhill confronts the professor, arguing against the way the Cold War is used to justify his methods. Thornhill is also represented as the victim of a situation that is secretly controlled by government authorities.

A number of themes overlap throughout the film: an innocent man on the run; his isolation; his transformation; romance; theatrical manipulation; and a secret world of espionage and international conflict.

space and time

As in many other Hitchcock films, the presentation of particular spaces contributes to suspense, shock and surprise within the narrative. Initially the film shows spaces that signify a safe, affluent world such as the Oak Bar in the hotel, where Thornhill meets his business associates. The dramatic intervention by Vandamm's henchmen is made more surprising because the location provides no suggestion that such a development will occur. The distinctive spaces that are introduced subsequently help to establish spectacular action and surprising juxtapositions. The businesslike atmosphere of the UN building is transformed by the sudden dramatic twist of Lester Townsend's murder. The knife thrown across the room is like a shocking circus stunt. The magnitude of the building helps to move the narrative on to a more extreme level of fantasy.

It has been noted that thrillers will often use the idea of a labyrinth, a space that becomes more convoluted as you pass deeper into it, and from which there appears to be no escape (Rubin, 1999, pp. 22–30). Hitchcock's

space and time — narrative & form

suspense, surprise and shock qualities

direction conveys the idea of spaces in which there is no clear idea of how the protagonist can escape. Repeatedly Thornhill appears to be trapped in particular locations: in the hotel lift; aboard the Twentieth Century Train; in the wide open prairie; and finally surrounded by the monuments of Mount Rushmore. These spaces are made into dangerous locations for the hero by the sudden appearance of his adversaries but also through effects achieved by editing and mise-en-scène (see Style: Mise-en-scène, Camerawork & Framing; and Editing).

The representation of time is also strongly related to the effects of suspense, surprise and shock qualities identified by Robin Wood as central in Hitchcock's cinema. The story takes place within a relatively short time span – it seems to occur across five or six days. The pacing of the film emphasises how particular situations move to their climax – the search for Lester Townsend culminates in his murder; the dramatic sequence on the train journey leads to the embrace between Thornhill and Eve, and the revelation that she is working for Vandamm. Our response to these sequences is focused on dramatic development instead of on a more objective sense of time. At critical points – such as when Thornhill is fleeing from the police and when he seeks to rescue Eve from Vandamm at the end – we are given the feeling that time is running out for the hero. In other words, in such sequences specific deadlines develop from the action to make suspense clear-cut and dominant.

equilibrium and disequilibrium

These concepts have been used to describe the way that many mainstream narratives appear to follow a general pattern. This involves first presenting the main characters in a situation of relative peace and security. Stability, however, is disrupted and **equilibrium** is restored fully only at the climax of the film. Like many general theories applied to individual narratives the idea of equilibrium and disequilibrium can seem inaccurate. A sense of disequilibrium can occur right at the beginning of a film. Also to assert that the climax re-establishes equilibrium may fail to address more

narrative & form — equilibrium...

reminiscent of an MGM musical

complex issues such as ambiguity within the narrative. However, it is worth considering briefly how *North by Northwest* appears to fit quite neatly with this account of a dominant approach to narrative structure.

As we have seen, Thornhill's world is thrown into crisis, creating questions for the viewer about how the narrative may develop. The sources of instability are fully defeated only when Leonard tumbles over the cliff and Thornhill lifts Eve to safety. At various points through the narrative a degree of equilibrium appears to have been restored. Thornhill's first escape from Vandamm's men is apparently a return to safety. Towards the end, Thornhill's meeting with the professor and later the meeting between Thornhill and Eve in the woods provide momentary suggestions that Thornhill has escaped but offer only partial respite from the central conflict that drives the narrative on. Thornhill repeatedly becomes involved in danger through a combination of factors but mainly due to his own motivation to combat the enemy and Vandamm's conviction that Thornhill is a key adversary. The experience of disequilibrium can be related then to the cause and effect structure of the narrative with its emphasis on character motivations (see Narrative & Form: Narrative Structure).

Classical Hollywood films predominantly seek to establish a strong sense of closure, which involves the triumph of good over evil and a full revelation of any undisclosed information relevant to understanding the main events of the narrative. The ending will also be affected by the conventions of whatever genres are being used. In *North by Northwest* the thriller, adventure and comedy genres determine a finale that is spectacular, and action based. It also contains witty lines and comic moments amidst the representation of danger threatening the hero and heroine. The Mount Rushmore location is used to give the final spectacle an original quality and refers loosely to the political theme of a struggle for national security. At one point, as the couple snake along the surface of the Mount Rushmore monument, the combination of their movements and the soundtrack is reminiscent of an MGM musical. Hitchcock and Lehman certainly approached the ending in an irreverent spirit. They wished, for example, to have Thornhill struck by a fit of sneezing while hiding inside Lincoln's nose.

equilibrium... narrative & form

ingenious, original style in the film form

It has been argued that heterosexual romance provides the dominant structure for achieving final equilibrium in Hollywood narrative irrespective of other themes introduced within the narrative. Thus the climax of the film leads to this ultimate resolution of the narrative. Here, however, the film-makers retain a light-hearted touch, **dissolving**, with a creative use of **match on action**, from Thornhill and Eve on the cliff-face to a single shot of the couple in the train. While the narrative clearly draws on the conventions of classical Hollywood it also provides the basis for ingenious, original style in the film form. The film concludes with a shot of the train entering the tunnel, which of course can be considered a cliché but also represents a humorous way to stand back from the Thornhill-Eve romance.

style

mise-en-scène, camerawork & framing *p37*   editing *p42*
sound effects *p48*

mise-en-scène, camerawork & framing

Originally applied to theatre, mise-en-scène became a vital concept for film critics who sought to show how the meaning of a particular movie may be enriched by the elements organised in front of the camera. Bordwell and Thompson define mise-en-scène as: 'All of the elements placed in front of the camera to be photographed: the settings and props, lighting, costumes and make-up, and figure behaviour' (Bordwell and Thompson, 2001, p. 432). A problem with discussing mise-en-scène in isolation is that the elements just listed are used to signify specific meanings in conjunction with all the other creative decisions involved in the making of the film, including the development of narrative, screenplay, and editing. Nevertheless Hitchcock's emphasis on the significance of the image within cinema indicates the value of looking closely at the contribution made by the mise-en-scène of particular shots to the film as a whole. We need to consider the power of individual images within the film, and effects achieved through the organisation of these images – including composition, framing and camerawork.

Some film-makers have self-consciously made the look of their film carry symbolic significance (for instance the distorted sets of the German expressionist film *The Cabinet of Dr Caligari*, released in 1919). In *North by Northwest* settings are used at a more supplementary level in relation to the action, enhancing the feeling of suspense. The confined spaces of the train build up the sense of tension as Thornhill seeks to escape from the police and in his meeting with Eve. The setting is also used to supplement themes such as Thornhill's isolation. In the prairie scene the wide open space enhances the emphasis on Thornhill's vulnerability.

mise-en-scène　　　　　　　　　　　　　　　　style

a minute figure dwarfed by the scale of the building

Camerawork is employed to give more impact to specific images. Before Thornhill is abducted, the camera moves in on the two villains. Framing also plays a vital role. The villains occupy the whole frame, blocking out most of the background. We are made aware of a threat to Thornhill before the real nature of the problem is clear. In a later scene one of these villains is revealed to the audience as the camera moves across to show the character who appears to be cutting a hedge as he turns to observe Thornhill leaving Townsend's house. In both cases camerawork highlights details that signify the threat to Thornhill.

Another example of camera movement used in this way occurs when Eve makes a telephone call from the Chicago train station. The camera moves across to reveal Leonard in a booth at the other end of the row. The decision to show this conversation in a single take again places dramatic emphasis on Thornhill's proximity to danger and the pervasive presence of Vandamm's gang. Although the camera movement here means that we are one step ahead of Thornhill, we are also deprived of knowledge, unable to hear the sinister clandestine plan being discussed.

Hitchcock achieves expressive effects through use of **high angle shots** The scene showing Thornhill's first meeting with Vandamm and Leonard involves a shot that suddenly makes us look down on the action, again emphasising Thornhill's vulnerability. Later the high angle extreme long shot of Thornhill escaping from the UN building conveys a further twist towards extremity in his situation. He is presented here as a minute figure dwarfed by the scale of the building. Since this shot immediately precedes the scene introducing the intelligence authorities, the use of a detached perspective also contributes to the idea of Thornhill as a pawn in their conflict with Vandamm.

The film develops dramatic intensity through shots that convey the sense of looking down from a disturbing height and shots that present confined spaces in which Thornhill is trapped. At the end of the film both of these approaches are brought together as Thornhill and Eve are trapped on the cliff edge.

Close-up and medium close-up develop the significance of particular objects within the story. When Thornhill investigates Kaplan's hotel room

style — mise-en-scène

visual details revealed through close camerawork

he finds a photograph showing Vandamm amidst an assembled group of people. Shown in close-up, this image contributes to the mysterious aura around Vandamm and the photograph is subsequently used by Thornhill in his visit to the United Nations when he tries to find Vandamm.

When Thornhill hides in Eve's bathroom on the train, a close-up of her razor in his hand introduces a prop that becomes key in the comic shaving scene later in the narrative. When Thornhill meets Eve in her hotel bedroom a shot from a detached perspective shows a gun in Eve's handbag, which Thornhill is unaware of. Moments later the close-up of a piece of notepaper, on which Thornhill manages to trace an address that Eve has written down, provides a vital clue allowing him to follow her to the auction room. Thus visual details revealed through close camerawork play a significant role in the narrative. It is notable here how Thornhill's point of view dominates, providing a justification for his actions.

The concept of a motif has been used in film studies to describe how an element in the film may become more prominent through repetition. At various points hands appear to be presented as a significant motif in *North by Northwest*. This may not be obvious until we consider the number of scenes that involve attention to characters' hands. When Eve and Thornhill converse at the dining table a shot that lingers on Thornhill lighting Eve's cigarette signifies the development of intimacy. Later, when they kiss in her cabin, Thornhill's hands on her shoulders convey the intensity of his desire. When Thornhill visits the auction, the scene begins with a medium close-up of Vandamm's hand on Eve's neck, which suggests a sinister form of possession. Finally, dramatic emphasis on hands plays a vital role at the climax as Thornhill clings on to Eve's hand on the rock face. The emphasis on this motif provides a visual focal point within the development of the narrative. Going back to the definition of mise-en-scène provided earlier, it is clear that Hitchcock thought carefully about how specific physical details could be foregrounded in a way that is both varied and consistent with the dominant themes of the narrative.

Colour plays a vivid role in the film as the narrative moves between locations. When *North by Northwest* was released one reviewer noted the expression of colours conveyed through the cinematography and praised

mise-en-scène   style

> shadow is used to imply threatening situations

cinematographer Robert Burks for depicting the 'hot yellows' of the prairie and 'the soft greens of South Dakota' (*Variety*, 1 July 1959).

To an extent colour plays a symbolic role. The contrast between Thornhill and various settings is developed as he continues to wear a grey suit, while Eve is made more visually striking in particular scenes through wearing red and later orange. We have suggested that, following the style of auteur theory, the film can be related to earlier parts of Hitchcock's career, but the use of colour gives the film immediately higher production values and contributes to the lavish feel of *North by Northwest*. Hitchcock's first film in technicolor was *Rope* made in 1948.

LIGHTING

A specific area for mise-en-scène analysis is lighting. The intention in the film is clearly not the search for lifelike qualities in a documentary style. Instead, Hitchcock aimed for a certain degree of **'realism'** through use of some locations in conjunction with a relatively consistent approach to lighting (see Hitchcock's remarks quoted in Director as Auteur). Lighting is used to present the action as clearly as possible, and contributes to the glamorous image of the main performers and occasionally to the spectacular quality of the fictional world depicted. We are not supposed to be distracted by consideration of how a scene has been lit. Instead the film fluidly combines scenes shot on location and in the studio. The lighting is controlled so that it is an integrated part of the film-making process, contributing to the presentation of the narrative and effects achieved through other aspects of film style.

Despite working in the thriller genre Hitchcock has not been strongly associated with film noir in which atmospheric **low-key lighting** played a prominent role. Certainly the suspense of key scenes uses the contrast between dark and light – the drunken driving **sequence** and the climactic scenes take place at night, which increases the emphasis on danger. Also, shadow is used to imply threatening situations at key points in the narrative. For instance, Thornhill's shadow is an aspect of the mise-en-scène as he tries to creep up on Vandamm, Leonard and Eve in the house. It is a discreet shadow and does not compete strongly for our attention

style — mise-en-scène

play on light and dark

with Thornhill's movements. Low-key illumination of this scene contributes nevertheless to the suspense. At the same time, since the shadow is not overtly stressed it is easier to assume that it is a consequence of the minimal lighting of the room that Thornhill moves through.

At earlier points shadow is also used to signify danger. An unobtrusive, but distinct shadow is cast from Thornhill on to the wall of the hotel room when he is searching for the evidence of George Kaplan. In an understated way this use of shadow reinforces the theme of Thornhill being haunted by a double. This expressive effect is not stressed. A more convincing explanation for the use of shadow towards the end is that it adds to the feeling of suspense. At the same time we may simply interpret the appearance of shadow at various points as a natural consequence of the lighting in the room.

The mixture of comedy and thriller evident in the drunken driving sequence means that the action does not take place within a very threatening level of darkness. Instead we see Thornhill well lit as he drives and the visual perspective of his point of view allows a clear representation of the road ahead, appearing as if illuminated by the car headlights. This sequence looks artificial due to **rear projection**: Thornhill in the car appears to be separated from the background. However, the play on light and dark in this sequence disguises an even more pronounced effect of artificiality. The lighting helps to concentrate our attention on Thornhill's expressions and the immediate background details. Rather than seeing the artificial quality of this sequence as a deficiency in the film-making, it can be argued that it works effectively in relation to the sense of an unreal situation that is both nightmarish and humorous (Debra Fried discusses and draws attention to the use of process shots in Hitchcock's American films – see Freedman and Millington in the Bibliography).

A Hitchcock film such as *Psycho*, with its powerful use of contrasting black and white, plunges us towards disturbing hidden terrors that could occur in reality. In contrast, *North by Northwest* is closer to a more playful state in which the boundaries between conscious and unconscious perceptions of reality are blurred.

mise-en-scène — style

lighting effects contribute to a sense of unease

It is striking that the film involves suspenseful and shocking narrative twists in scenes set in broad daylight. Of course many film noirs also include such an approach but with *North by Northwest* we can see a particular focus on a surprising collision between ordinary life and danger. This leads to a rejection of the formulaic use of low-key lighting for suspense.

The discreet emphasis on depicting lighting sources within the mise-en-scène helps to develop our suspension of disbelief. The scene in which Thornhill first meets Vandamm, and the scene when Thornhill and Eve are in the hotel bedroom in Chicago involve shots in which lamps are strategically allowed some prominence as part of the furniture. William Rothman discusses how the lighting, alongside other props, has an impact on the way Eve is presented in this scene (for further details of Rothman's analysis see Critical Responses). In the first scene the shadow that falls on Vandamm's face and the way light falls on Thornhill provide another instance of how lighting effects depicted within the mise-en-scène contribute to a sense of unease. We may dismiss the representation of light sources within the scene as incidental detail, but lighting is also an integral element in dramatic action. Hitchcock keeps us alive to the key role of lighting within films, but like other film-makers working in commercial cinema he concentrates our attention on the mise-en-scène rather than on the film-making process itself.

editing

A subject that has promoted debate in relation to many films is the question of whether editing is effective when the action could be shown within a single shot. Editing is used frequently to present characters' actions or speech in separate shots while they occupy a single space. The scale of the shot may provide emotional emphasis. Medium close-ups and close-ups used in a **shot/reverse shot** pattern to depict a conversation will provide specific details of each character's behaviour and emotions. This convention is a vital element in **continuity editing**

Editing is sometimes used as an expressive device when the action could have been shown without a cut. In the opening sections of *North by*

style editing

emphasis on Thornhill's subjective state

Northwest shots are relatively brief throughout, isolating individual actions in the excitement of the event that unfolds. When Thornhill is taken hostage he is shown in a cramped position, hemmed in by the two men. He breaks from talking to them by trying to make a quick exit through the door of the car. At this point there is a **match on action** to show the abrupt nature of the escape attempt.

Thornhill's predicament is accentuated by emphasis on his point of view. During the car journey the surroundings of the country house are introduced through shots that represent his perception of this new environment. Framed by the window of the car these shots maintain the focus on his situation as a prisoner. Arguably the **point of view shots** develop the spectator's identification with Thornhill and contribute significantly to continuity since these shots are smoothly incorporated within the action.

When Thornhill meets Vandamm the exchange involves a shot/reverse shot pattern. This is given a more specific style as both characters move around the room. The editing juxtaposes the movements of the camera tracking the actions of each character, and thus enhances the feeling of disorientation and confrontation between the protagonist and the chief villain.

In the drunken driving sequence some shots are connected by **dissolves**, with a short period in which shots which are **superimposed**. The dissolves reinforce the idea that this sequence presents a condensed version of the journey, but also contribute to the emphasis on Thornhill's subjective state, half conscious and still drunk. The editing works with the non-diegetic music (see Sound Effects) through this sequence to convey his experience but also the soundtrack expressively represents the drama of the journey at a more abstract level.

Understatement is frequently a characteristic of the film's style, working alongside the spectacular nature of certain scenes. At the level of editing, an example of this understatement is the way minor characters are depicted economically. For example, amongst the various car journeys shown, shots are included to represent the verbal exchanges that take place. When Thornhill is driven to the United Nations in a taxi we might

editing style

motif of the dangerous, anonymous stranger

expect the driver to be revealed as another agent conspiring to trap him after the shocks that have already been introduced. By including a shot of the driver's head seen by Thornhill from the back seat Hitchcock allows the possibility of an eerie sense that this unidentified individual may pose a threat. However, the film does not evolve towards being a conspiracy thriller. The minor characters who are not villains are represented to provide background detail and maintain the sense that an ordinary world continues away from the central drama, and they play a role in scenes that involve comic, ironic qualities such as the two occasions on which Thornhill is arrested.

The motif of the dangerous, anonymous stranger returns in the crop-dusting scene when the pilot who attacks Thornhill is not identified. The decision not to show the assassin relates to the way in which the film achieves intensity through concentration on selected details. Another instance of this occurs during the train journey sequence when only four shots show a perspective from outside the train and even these are restricted to a camera position on the side of the train.

Certain shots achieve a subtle level of disorientation in relation to the story. The first shot taken from the edge of the train is followed by a camera movement into the carriage. In this way the editing intermittently allows a sense of an omipresent perspective where we are made more conscious of the active role played by the camerawork in revealing different visual perspectives. Another example occurs when Eve and Thornhill embrace in her carriage and this is shown from a position that, viewed from another angle, seems impossible due to the location of the wall. In other words, the film appears momentarily to heighten our sense of artifice in what is depicted. Another interpretation is that we are simply disorientated at a subliminal level by the surprising angle introduced at this point.

THE CROP-DUSTING SCENE

This famous episode occurs after a scene in which Thornhill says goodbye to Eve Kendall. The transition from one location to the next is achieved with a dissolve from Eve, whose face initially reveals some distress before becoming composed. This image dissolves to a high angle establishing shot

style   editing

a lull before the action begins

of the deserted road with the bus arriving. The dissolve conveys the idea of a hidden connection between Eve and the destiny that awaits Thornhill in this new scenario. It also can be interpreted as signifying that Eve is thinking about Thornhill. The relationship between the two characters is ambiguous. Eve has been forced to send Thornhill to this situation and the final shots of her before this event may briefly indicate buried feelings of conflict.

The crop-dusting scene is extraordinarily dramatic, involving spectacular action, and suspense developed through silence, specific isolated sounds and minimal dialogue. In this section we will concentrate on how editing, in conjunction with camerawork, mise-en-scène, screenplay, acting and framing, achieves specific effects.

The establishing shot is maintained for a considerable length with a cut introduced only after the bus delivering Thornhill to this spot has departed out of the frame and can no longer be heard. The length of the shot provides a lull before the action begins. It allows the viewer to comprehend the deserted nature of the area where Thornhill waits. The second shot is sufficiently close to identify Thornhill, but is also distant enough to repeat the image of empty space around him. From a **low angle** the second shot provides some disorientation after the high angle perspective. We see Thornhill almost in profile, a visual perspective that provides variation. This set-up also makes the character stand out from the background. The juxtaposition develops the theme of an innocent character struggling in an environment that contains hidden dangers. Still wearing his grey suit, Thornhill is conspicuously out of place in this setting. The shots that follow alternate between Thornhill looking and what he sees, although this correspondence is not exact because the angle from which the landscape is depicted only approximates the angle from which he looks. The relationship between the direction of Thornhill's look and the visual perspective depicting the landscape is edgy as Thornhill keeps moving impatiently. Two cars arrive and depart, with a range of shots indicating Thornhill's look and the passing of each car. When a lorry sends a cloud of dust in Thornhill's direction a change of angle is used to show it passing him and there is no shot to depict its departure over the horizon. The style here provides a variation in the build-up of frustration.

editing
style

emphasis on physical expression

The lack of knowledge about which direction Kaplan may appear from leads on to the way space is organised when the plane attacks from various directions. Before this occurs, Thornhill notices a car approaching from the track opposite. He becomes more and more expectant that it may contain Kaplan. When a man emerges from the car, a shot of both characters in profile, in the mid-distance, with their hands near their hips, heightens the drama of the meeting at a purely visual level. Thornhill then decides to approach the stranger. Here the editing provides a repetition of Thornhill looking and his point of view of a particular subject with two travelling point of view shots conveying his approach to the figure who Thornhill hopes will be Kaplan.

When it is made clear by the man that he is not Kaplan, the presence of the crop-duster plane is introduced. Speaking with Truffaut about this moment, Hitchcock insisted on the necessity of showing the plane initially from a perspective that was not Thornhill's point of view. In this way we get the idea that the plane is simply a normal part of the location. As Hitchcock points out, he used the same approach in *The Birds* (1963) when we see the bird that attacks before it is seen by the main protagonist. In that film the attack is more sudden. In *North by Northwest* the stranger sees the plane first. His remark on the incongruity of the plane's presence, as he claims that there are no crops to be sprayed, provides a cue for the explosive action that follows. When the stranger departs on the bus, the sense of frustration experienced by Thornhill at this latest disappointment is overridden by the returning emphasis on his solitary position, cut off from help.

In the scene as a whole our attention is drawn to Thornhill's reactions to what he sees. As the plane attacks, the camera records even more closely his reactions, which naturally are more extreme. His apparently futile struggle is represented graphically as he attempts to run away as the plane bears down. Thornhill desperately gestures for a car to stop but is unable to communicate the ordeal he faces. Again one is reminded here of Hitchcock's experience in silent cinema, with the emphasis on physical expression in the acting. From here the editing is guided principally by the action, with separate shots depicting such elements of the drama as

| style | editing |

> a close-up showing Thornhill falling under the lorry

Thornhill diving to the ground; Thornhill struggling into a small desolate section of crops; and, throughout, the plane's various lines of attack. As Thornhill hides amidst the crops one visual perspective included involves the camera in a low angle position outside the hiding place. We are given a view here that reveals what Thornhill cannot see. The whole sequence relies on oscillation between his point of view and shots that observe his plight in this life-and-death situation. These more detached shots also allow visual composition to carry the drama more forcefully as we see the plane diving down towards the crops.

After the plane has swooped over his hiding place, Thornhill runs to the road and this time stands right in the middle of the road gesturing for an oil lorry to halt. Here point of view and reaction shots reach a climax in a close-up showing Thornhill falling under the lorry as it pulls to a stop. In the split-second timing of this we may mistakenly feel that Thornhill has fainted or collided with the lorry. The theme of an accidental disaster is compounded as the plane crashes into the tanker. Thornhill hears the men from the tanker warning him about the explosion and runs to safety, then departs in a truck belonging to one of the onlookers who have arrived at the scene.

The sequence could have been shown in fewer shots. However, the even length of the shots builds a rhythm allowing Hitchcock to synthesise the initial sense of unease with the subsequent chain of abrupt shocks. Truffaut draws attention to the even length of the shots in his interview with Hitchcock, who replies by saying that the length of each shot was determined primarily by the aim of showing the distance travelled by Thornhill as the plane attacks and that Thornhill had nowhere to hide (Truffaut, 1966, pp. 387-9). Hitchcock also suggested that the audience would initially feel that Thornhill might be attacked by a passing car or lorry (Hitchcock, 1963, Cinema 1, no.5, in Gottlieb (ed.), 1997, p. 287). The scene achieves a powerful level of absurdity, drawing the audience in with the extended absence of dialogue and the explosive action. We are not told why Vandamm has selected such an elaborate method for assassinating Thornhill, but, at an abstract level, it represents Vandamm's excessive sadism. The scene can be related to later Hitchcock films such as *Psycho* and *The*

editing   style

dialogue, music and sound effects

Birds where sudden attacks on innocent characters are presented in a much more disturbing way.

sound effects

The soundtrack includes dialogue, music and sound effects. Since dialogue has featured in discussion of the narrative, we will start by briefly describing how isolated moments of dialogue occasionally acquire a particular significance through their position in the film.

Although the dialogue works mainly through conversations and verbal exchanges, there are points at which a single sentence or phrase is given dramatic emphasis. When Thornhill is forced to drink bourbon Leonard is heard saying 'cheers', an ironic phrase in the situation, which is followed by a **dissolve** to a shot that shows Thornhill being forced into a car. Leonard's ironic phrase might have been the last word that Thornhill heard before death and works alongside the dissolve to convey Thornhill's disturbing loss of consciousness. In the car Thornhill is unaware of the danger he faces. At this point music becomes prominent, signifying the escalation of danger.

Perhaps the most striking effect achieved by an isolated section of dialogue occurs in the crop-dusting scene. The minimal exchange between Thornhill and the stranger divides the scene between the passage where Thornhill waits and the attack of the plane. As well as drawing attention to the plane, the stranger's slightly morbid observation that some of the crop-duster pilots will get rich if they live long enough contributes to the sense of unease.

When the intelligence authorities decide they cannot help Thornhill, a woman in the group is shown saying plaintively 'goodbye Mr Thornhill, wherever you are'. Here the dialogue cues a switch in the action back to Thornhill but also carries a dream-like connotation of his helplessness. Like Leonard's false bonhomie, an isolated statement signifies the drama of Thornhill's position as a victim.

Music plays an important role right from the beginning of *North by Northwest*. As Royal S. Brown observes in his study of film music, the

style

sound effects

music is used as non-diegetic narration

soundtrack heard over the credits sequence in *North by Northwest* has a 'strong rhythmic drive' (Royal S. Brown, 1994, p. 69). Immediately the music conveys the fast pace of the narrative and a heightened mood so that we are arguably prepared at a subliminal level for the transition to unusual, bizarre events. Later the music is used to express suspense during action scenes and at various points is suddenly introduced in anticipation of a threat posed by the villains. For instance, when Thornhill and his mother are forced to leave the investigation of Kaplan's hotel room, with Vandamm's men in pursuit, the suspenseful music develops the tension, reminding us of the earlier attempt on Thornhill's life. Dialogue takes over as Thornhill's mother questions the men, and the crowd in the lift join in the laughter when the men treat her question as absurd. Although this sound is not marked as subjective it does convey an expressionistic feeling of Thornhill's private nightmare because the laughter becomes momentarily a dominant sound. Incidentally, Thornhill escapes from this situation with quick thinking and verbal ingenuity.

At certain points music is used in conjunction with a style of rapid editing in which common elements on a general theme are represented. This **montage** style is evident at the beginning with various shots depicting city crowds. When Thornhill drives drunk, the music unifies a sequence in which various shots juxtapose different stages in the journey. The arrival at Chicago involves a humorous sequence of shots depicting porters with red caps, with the soundtrack providing an accompaniment.

Throughout the film, music is used as non-diegetic narration. This means that it is not shown to come from sources within the fictional world, but instead plays an expressive role, developing mood and atmosphere. However, when Eve and Thornhill are at the dining table on the train the soundtrack provides music that is represented as part of the fictional world. The music here contributes to the idea of a relaxed ambience aboard the train conducive to easy conversation and the flirtatious exchanges between Eve and Thornhill. The composer Herrmann creates a transition from this diegetic musical background to romantic theme music and finally the more suspenseful non-diegetic music that follows when Thornhill sees the police approaching the train. The music provides a

sound effects *style*

an unusual sound effect

background along with the sound of the train as our attention focuses on the exchange between the two characters.

The decision about when to use music and when to rely purely on silence and sound effects contributes to the film's main themes. When Thornhill sees Eve again at the hotel in Chicago the quietness seems to express her role as a femme fatale. Thornhill now associates Eve with the attempt on his life. Her presence in the hotel is enigmatic and not precisely explained by the narrative. When they meet again after Thornhill has followed Eve to her room, the music is initially romantic. This reflects Eve's relief that he has survived and the music seems to override the suspicion Thornhill now holds in relation to her actions. This is an example of the way the music is used intermittently to put greater emphasis on mood and atmosphere rather than allowing clear, precise explanation of the narrative.

At the outset of the crop-dusting scene, the isolated sounds of cars passing and then the sound of the plane and the firing of ammunition are made prominent, in conjunction with the use of silence. In a later scene, an unusual sound effect occurs as the professor seeks to explain to Thornhill how he has become embroiled in a conflict relating to national security. The conversation is made inaudible briefly due to the sound of the nearby aeroplanes. In his interview with Hitchcock, Truffaut raises this effect as a subject for discussion. As Truffaut points out, the audience are not deprived of vital information by the intrusion of the sound effect since the earlier scene with the security service provided some explanation of the conflict with Vandamm. However, Truffaut continues his appreciation of this sound effect suggesting that, '... it makes us lose all notion of time. The counter-intelligence man [the professor] spends thirty seconds in telling Cary Grant a story that, in reality, would take him, at the very least, three minutes to tell' (Truffaut, 1966, p. 382).

contexts

ideology *p51* **film contexts** *p57* **other cultural contexts** *p66*
critical responses *p68* **the audience** *p71*

ideology

Although definitions of ideology have varied, a consistent meaning conveyed by this concept is that certain ideas and beliefs are made to seem natural when they appear in forms of culture such as cinema. Since we usually watch narrative cinema as entertainment or as art we may uncritically accept ideas about the world and human nature that the film contains. Describing such ideas as an ideology or as ideological suggests that they convey specific values that are open to debate. To discuss the ideology of a film therefore involves recognising how the film may present stereotypes or pervasive ideas about people and society. Alternatively, discussion of ideology may involve showing how a film challenges influential ideas within society or ideas maintained by other film-makers.

Relating a film to dominant ideas within the society in which it is produced can be difficult. Although *North by Northwest* contains elements of the political thriller and at specific points evokes the context of the Cold War, the film does not seek to comment explicitly on contemporary politics. One interpretation is that the film provides an indirect critique of the political repression that occurred in the USA when Senator McCarthy sought to expel communist sympathisers from Hollywood. McCarthy's persecution of communists was recognised to be a witch-hunt, a ruthless policy governed by a right-wing response to the tension in relations between the USA and the USSR.

Although *North by Northwest* provides no parallel to the events involving McCarthy, the film does convey the feeling that innocent people may be oppressed in a political policy governed by the requirements of the Cold War. Also the film contains oblique references to the infamous Alger Hiss case. Hiss was a respected American public official who was accused of giving government secrets to a secret communist organisation in 1948 by

ideology   contexts

> innocent people can be embroiled in political conflict

Whittaker Chambers, who had already admitted to working for the communists. Chambers sought to prove his accusations by showing microfilms of papers. He claimed that these papers were government secrets that Hiss planned to transport to the Soviet Union and that had been hidden inside a hollowed-out pumpkin. Hiss was sentenced to five years' imprisonment but subsequently evidence was brought forward to suggest that he had been the victim of the purging tactics of McCarthy and corrupt treatment of evidence by the FBI. (These details of the Alger Hiss case are provided by an entry in Drexel, *Facts on File Encyclopedia of the Twentieth Century*.) With the reference to Vandamm's African statuette by Thornhill as the pumpkin it can be argued that *North by Northwest* raised the issue of the Hiss case (Richard Millington draws attention to this in his analysis of the film – see Bibliography). Through Townsend's death and Thornhill's trials and tribulations there is a suggestion of how innocent people can be embroiled in political conflict with the secret services playing a shady role.

However, a more striking feature of the film is the fact that no political ideas are strongly developed. Hitchcock after all described the depiction of espionage activities as ultimately a ploy to develop the narrative. Potential political content is systematically presented in a way that avoids direct reference to actual issues. Vandamm is not even provided with a nationality, but operates as an apparently freelance destabiliser of national security.

The attack on those with left wing beliefs in Hollywood had receded after McCarthy lost office in 1954. Nevertheless it can still be argued that the context of the Cold War was having an indirect effect on Hollywood film-making in 1959. *North by Northwest* seeks to avoid explicit political comment, yet it is interesting to examine how the film is influenced by this context. On the one hand the character of Vandamm could be regarded as providing a stereotypical representation of the outsider who infiltrates a safe, affluent society. On the other hand, the film shows a liberal approach with its absurdist sense of humour and Thornhill's ultimate defiance of the intelligence authorities.

The context of a spy story provides a neat basis for concentrating on the idea of role-play. Role-play is used as a source of entertainment through

contexts ideology

world of deceptive appearances

the theme of theatricality. It can be argued that this theme relates to an increasing awareness in American society that identity and social actions might be determined by role-play or fabrication. This is already suggested by Thornhill's profession as an advertising man, which he says depends on the art of exaggeration. However, the film does not develop a message about this issue. Thornhill gets involved in a more intense, serious world of deceptive appearances through a complete accident. Also, despite the evident ruthlessness of the intelligence authorities, who are not prepared initially to save Thornhill, the film does not unequivocally criticise counter-espionage activities. Instead, Hitchcock and Lehman simply drew on increasing public awareness of the role played by espionage in American society in the 1950s.

The FBI (the Federal Bureau of Investigation) was started in 1908. Following the Second World War and the perceived threat posed by the USSR, special provisions for counter-espionage work in America had been instituted in 1947 through the National Security Act with the establishment of the CIA (Central Intelligence Agency). During the 1950s the number of employees working for the CIA increased enormously, with agents masquerading behind many different professional roles, from government officials to businessmen and -women (a development discussed by Engelhardt – see Bibliography). When the film presents the group in a meeting with the professor close to the White House it is striking that they are shown as ordinary people. Although the film may present a feeling of incredulity about their operations it also tones down the sense of sinister secretive operations impinging on the public. The presentation of these characters as ordinary also indicates the recognition of work by the security services in relation to American daily life.

In the late 1950s the threat to American society by an enemy within was portrayed by certain films in a way that was both abstract and clearly ideological. For instance, the aliens in *Invasion of the Body Snatchers* (Don Siegel, 1956) have been interpreted as representing the threat of communism and at the least a fear that individualism was threatened by an impersonal mass society. (For a full development of this argument in relation to American cinema of the 1950s see Biskind, 1983.) Hitchcock

ideology

a fascination with a symbolic threat

and Lehman do not follow this tendency. On the one hand it can be argued that the theme of theatricality in *North by Northwest* allows crude ideas about the enemy within to be satirised through humour. Vandamm is almost self-consciously presented as an archetypal villain relating to conventions within crime fiction. At the end he protests that the professor has used 'real bullets' to kill Leonard, a line that again suggests the theme of theatricality, but that also may represent Vandamm's ironic and arrogant lack of concern as his loyal agent dies. On the other hand, the fact that Vandamm is not precisely developed as a character, is connected with a mysterious organisation, and is associated with the Cold War maintains the idea of the enemy within. It can be argued that through the character of Vandamm the film plays on a fascination with a symbolic threat that is not realistically defined.

GENDER

The concept of ideology can also be applied to discussion of the way gender is presented in *North by Northwest*. In the section Director as Auteur, we introduced ideas that may be used to challenge emphasis on the creativity of Hitchcock. Instead of celebrating his skill as a director, analysis can focus on the way film form is used to present gender in a stereotypical fashion. In Characterisation we touched on how the film develops the Cary Grant character more extensively than the female protagonist.

Hitchcock's films have been analysed by feminist film theorists such as Laura Mulvey and Tania Modleski to produce a range of different perspectives. This work has been concerned not just with the content of the films but with how they reproduce dominant ideas. Hitchcock's films replicate some of the general elements of Hollywood cinema discussed in work on narrative and film form. For example, *North by Northwest*, like many other commercial narrative films, relies on suspension of disbelief by the viewer. This is cultivated by the style of the film. Conventions such as **continuity editing** allow a story to unfold in which the main protagonist heroically confronts evil, without appearing to demand too much critical thought from the audience.

contexts ideology

objects of desire and figures of danger

The story also reinforces the stereotypical presentation of the female character as an object of desire for the hero (however, see Rothman's analysis, briefly summarised in Critical Responses, which provides a slightly different perspective). *North by Northwest* reproduces a dominant pattern in Hollywood cinema, favouring the main male character with a storyline centred on his actions and a preponderance of shots from his point of view. It is only through Thornhill's actions that the possibility of rescuing Eve arises. In a most obvious way the film presents a stereotypical story of the virtuous man and ultimately a woman who is made increasingly passive by the situation depicted.

However, feminist film theory has also made discussion of Hitchcock's films much more complex. This has been due partly to the role played by psychoanalytical ideas in analysis of the films. Psychoanalytical concepts have been used to explore why female characters are frequently set up as both objects of desire and figures of danger. One argument is that the threat of difference presented by the woman is played out in the life-and-death struggle of the male protagonist. Her power to represent difference must be subdued through assertion of male control, and/or she must become involved in a union with the male character (see Creed, in Hill and Church (eds), 1998, for further discussion of related issues). *Vertigo* provides an example of how the threat posed by the female character may be resolved through punishment and annihilation. The hero is obsessed with the woman. Ultimately he brings her under his control and she is punished with death, although he does not intend this to happen (see Film Contexts: Filmography). In *North by Northwest* Eve comes close to the fate suffered by Judy at the end of *Vertigo*, but of course the intervention of the security services allows Thornhill to rescue her.

Feminist film theory has also made the analysis of ideology in Hitchcock's work more complex by recognising that the films often present gender in an ambivalent way. While the female character may frequently be made more passive towards the end of the narrative, in many films directed by Hitchcock the presentation of gender is more complicated because of changes that occur during the course of the story. Tania Modleski draws our attention to the way in which the O at the centre of Roger's name

ideology

assertion of power through the male protagonist

evokes a sense of uncertainty at the heart of his personality (Modleski, 1988, p. 91). Despite the development of his status as a hero, towards the end the film concentrates significantly on the male character as a victim. The pattern of moving between his point of view and shots that represent the danger to him is maintained for so much of the film that suspense dominates over assertion of power through his actions. For a significant part of the film Eve and Thornhill are both presented as victims.

There are other factors that make the assertion of power through the male protagonist more complicated in films directed by Hitchcock. Most obviously, his films depict individual male characters as the villains. Again *Vertigo* is useful as a graphic example. In this film Judy is ultimately controlled by the male villain. In *North by Northwest* Eve is restricted in her actions by her role as double agent, which involves appearing to act for Vandamm and ultimately obeying the commands of the professor.

Ambivalence is also associated with Hitchcock's direction in narratives in which villains are frequently given characteristics allowing some sympathy, or at least fascination with their actions on the part of the audience. Although we do not sympathise with Vandamm he displays qualities, such as his association with culture and his sophisticated manner, that give an indication of how the criminal may be a more ambiguous figure. *Blackmail* illustrates how Hitchcock's films may complicate our orientation to law and order. Released in 1929, the film shows the female protagonist kill a man who attempts to rape her and the rest of the story concentrates on her situation. In other Hitchcock films, criminals have been portrayed through strong characterisation. It appears then that *North by Northwest* is less ambivalent in this respect but continues to play with our instinct to favour law and order by showing Thornhill pursued by the police.

It can be argued that shots representing the point of view of the male protagonist unconsciously and uncritically display a way in which male dominance is frequently maintained by narrative films. Films such as *Rear Window* and *Vertigo* bring to the fore the male hero's reliance on hidden observation, and to a limited degree this is repeated in *North by Northwest* when Thornhill follows Eve to the auction. In many other Hollywood films the dominance of the male character's point of view is critical to our

contexts

film contexts

Hitchcock developed semi-independent status

sympathy for his position, but we are made less aware of the relationship between power and the look. Hitchcock's male protagonists are rendered more complex through the obsessive qualities involved in their actions, including their visual observations. Thus such films may be criticised for establishing an intense identification between the viewer and the male character working alongside the perspective of the male direction. However, the degree of dependence on point of view in these films may unintentionally make a spectator more aware of how the film guides perception. *North by Northwest* to an extent typifies a predominantly male perspective, but the way in which this perspective develops, with the emphasis on entertainment and absurdity, means that how the audience read the narrative is still open to debate.

film contexts

THE INDUSTRY

In one chapter of his book *The Genius of the System*, Thomas Schatz includes discussion of the relationship between Hitchcock and the Hollywood film industry. Schatz describes how Hitchcock acquired independence as a director while the power of the studios was declining. After his own independent production company had failed commercially, Hitchcock still developed semi-independent status. His own production team on a variety of films in the 1950s included, for instance, George Tomasini as editor, Robert Burks responsible for photography and Robert Boyle designing film sets. Through the 1950s Hitchcock increasingly directed films in technicolor and using VistaVision, a widescreen process. *North by Northwest* builds on the run of films directed by Hitchcock in the early 1950s ranging from *Strangers on a Train* (1951) to *Rear Window* (1954) in which a medium-scale budget and use of popular stars contributed to box-office success. *North by Northwest* involved an increase in budget and relied on the star power of Cary Grant.

Hollywood film production since the beginning of the studio system had included films marked out by the use of particularly popular stars and lavish production values, but in the 1950s star blockbusters became more

film contexts

dependence on independent production

significant as a way of differentiating cinema from the competition provided by television. *North by Northwest* was planned to cost $3.1 million, significantly more expensive than the average Hollywood film. Eventually the film's cost escalated to $4.3 million. This contrasts with *Vertigo* made the previous year for $2.3 million and *Psycho* made the following year for $0.8 million. Previously Hitchcock's most expensive film had been *The Paradine Case*, made in 1947 for $4 million, which had failed at the box office. (For full details of budgets and box-office returns, see Finler, 1992.)

The Hollywood studios had been forced to confront change following legislation introduced in 1948 which sought to prevent their control over exhibition and distribution. In response to this legislation MGM was the last studio to sell off their prestigious first-run theatres. During the 1930s and 1940s the studio had gained a reputation for making films that were more expensive than those of other studios. Although MGM's profits declined through the 1950s with the selling of their theatres, the studio continued to have some success. This was partly due to the quality of the musicals produced at MGM during this decade. Nevertheless when Hitchcock was signed by MGM as a director for a one-off film in 1957 the studio was in a position that seemed quite insecure compared to the height of the classical era. As Leonard J. Leff shows, between 1955 and 1960 MGM's dependence on independent production increased from 10 per cent to 80 per cent of its overall production (Leff in Deutelbaum and Poague (eds), 1986, p. 41). The signing of Hitchcock without the guarantee of any future work by the director is a good example of MGM's increasing reliance on films organised on an individual basis. *North by Northwest* was first shown in Chicago's United Artists Theatre on 1 July 1959. Partly due to the success of this film MGM profits rose dramatically in this year.

PRODUCTION HISTORY

Leff's article *Hitchcock at Metro* provides a detailed account of the production of *North by Northwest* and the relationship between Hitchcock and MGM through this process. Leff was able to consult documents from the studio and interview people involved who were still alive. Here we will briefly summarise some of the details that emerge from Leff's account of the production history, drawing where appropriate on other sources such

contexts | **film contexts**

the title of the film changed

as Lehman's introduction to the published version of the screenplay and the interviews with Hitchcock.

Hitchcock had been engaged by MGM to make a film version of *The Wreck of The Mary Deare*, a thriller by Hammond Innes. The film composer Bernard Herrmann, who had worked with Hitchcock already, introduced the director to Lehman who was already employed by MGM. Lehman was enthusiastic about working with Hitchcock but sceptical whether a film version of *The Wreck of The Mary Deare* would succeed. After various meetings in which an alternative idea evolved, Hitchcock and Lehman confronted the MGM executives with their plans for a different film, known initially as 'In a Northwesterly Direction'.

Lehman developed the narrative outline, frequently discussing ideas with Hitchcock who was also involved in pre-production plans for *Vertigo*. Lehman describes how he and Hitchcock developed the idea for the crop-duster scene in Hitchcock's living room. When Hitchcock left to work on *Vertigo*, Lehman continued, researching locations and later writing the screenplay at his MGM office. An important breakthrough in this process was Lehman's idea of the fake shooting, which allowed him to progress to the final Act of the story. The title of the film changed at various points. At one stage it was going to be called 'Breathless'. Later Hitchcock and Lehman agreed on calling it 'The Man in Lincoln's Nose' (Leff in Deutelbaum and Poague (eds), 1986, p. 41).

In order to succeed at the box office, *North by Northwest* required approval from the Production Code Association (PCA), who vetoed films on the basis of unacceptable language, the representation of sex, and material that might cause offence. At the outset, the board was concerned that the screenplay conveyed the idea that Eve was Vandamm's mistress and also worried that Leonard was depicted as gay. Although MGM executives feared that Hitchcock would not comply with the demands of the PCA, the director did make relevant changes. Thus at the end Thornhill and Eve are married and, for example, the word 'sweetie' was eliminated from Leonard's dialogue (Leff in Deutelbaum and Poague (eds), 1986, p. 52).

Various problems arose regarding locations specified in the screenplay. The United Nations would not allow the scene of Townsend's murder to be

film contexts

objection to use of the monument

filmed in the delegates' lounge, but Hitchcock and a photographer were given permission to take still pictures inside, from which Robert Boyle created a set. Great care was taken to reproduce the location as exactly as possible. The sequence also includes a scene involving a candid camera shot of the outside of the building when Cary Grant arrives. In the case of Mount Rushmore there was objection to use of the monument for filming from both the South Dakota Parks authorities and the US Department of Interior who stated that it would be 'patent desecration'. The location manager Charles Coleman attempted to negotiate for filming of the monument. Coleman wrote to the Parks authorities describing the film's use of Mount Rushmore in the following way: 'In the end, the enemies of democracy are defeated by the shrine of democracy' (Leff in Deutelbaum and Poague (eds), 1986, p. 51). However, they were not given permission to shoot action with the presidents' heads included in the shot. Robert Boyle adapted to this problem by creating the faces in the MGM studios. A miniature of the house designed by Frank Lloyd Wright was used to represent Vandamm's secret point of departure from the country.

As Hitchcock tells Truffaut in the 1966 interview, it was necessary for him to insist, against the wishes of the studio, on including the reconciliation scene in the forest between Eve and Thornhill (Truffaut, 1966, pp. 382–3). Eventually the studio fully supported the scene to the extent of acquiring trees from South Dakota for the studio set. MGM were also anxious that the film was going to exceed budget and Hitchcock was forced to ensure that the final scenes did not become excessively extravagant. At the same time *Ben-Hur*, another MGM production, eventually costing $16 million, was absorbing the studio's finances. The final part of *North by Northwest* to be completed was the credits sequence designed by Saul Bass.

VISTAVISION

VistaVision emerged as a rival screen format to cinemascope and cinerama in the early 1950s. VistaVision is another example of how Hollywood cinema sought to make cinema more distinctive to cope with the threat of competition from television. The film historian Gordon Gow describes the different effect offered by VistaVision:

contexts film contexts

> the first MGM film to be made using this format
>
> Generally shown in proportions nearer to the old screens, about twice as wide as its height, it could in fact be extremely high and therefore give the impression, when seen at its best, of a Cinemascope screen from which a top border had been hauled up to give more space.
>
> *Gow, 1971, p. 24*

Gow makes the point that VistaVision had advantages over cinemascope for close-ups and visual design of the image. The significance of particular close-ups in *North by Northwest* for suspense or concentration on a character's face made this a good format for the film. Also the emphasis on height in VistaVision was suitable for a film that repeatedly involves the viewer in high angle and overhead shots designed to startle or surprise. Hitchcock had gained experience of directing with the VistaVision process in his work for Paramount, starting with *To Catch a Thief* in 1955. However, *North by Northwest* was the first MGM film to be made using this format. Gow discusses some of the advantages and disadvantages of VistaVision as a new process in relation to exhibition. Many cinemas at the time were unable to show a film in the proportions of VistaVision. Although these cinemas had to reduce the film to 35mm, the size of the image could be reinstated during projection through use of an enlarging lens. However, this adaptation provided images that were less clearly defined than those achieved in the original VistaVision format (Gow, 1971, p. 24).

The introduction of wider and higher screens during the 1950s encouraged film-makers to put more emphasis on visual qualities offered by the location or set. The spectacular display of scenery was an advantage that cinema had over television. Discussing his work, Hitchcock remarks on the need to create the right balance between the effects achieved by the setting and concentration on the action (Gow, 1971, p. 27). It is not surprising then to find that *North by Northwest* was developed around sequences in which locations play a major role while our attention is focused on narrative development through character actions.

FILMOGRAPHY

The theoretical approached introduced by auteur critics encourages comparisons to be made across a director's range of films. In the case of

film contexts

twists and turns in a romantic relationship

Hitchcock and *North by Northwest* this approach is easy to justify since immediate, striking parallels emerge with many of the director's other films. *Saboteur* (1942) provides a clear precedent and contrast with the cliff-top ending of *North by Northwest*. At the end of *Saboteur* the hero clutches on to the villain's arm as the latter is just about to fall from the Statue of Liberty.

Auteurist approaches have included attempts to subdivide Hitchcock's films into particular groups. *North by Northwest* can be related to other Hitchcock films in which an innocent man is on the run. Alternatively *North by Northwest* may be grouped with *Vertigo* and *Psycho* (a grouping suggested by Spoto) because these three films were made at a specific juncture in Hitchcock's career and arguably can be compared for the way a feeling of bleakness is developed. Another approach would be to relate *North by Northwest* to other Hitchcock films starring Cary Grant.

In this section we will briefly examine points of contrast and comparison between *North by Northwest* and three films made by the director at different points in his career, concentrating primarily on aspects of the narrative.

Made in 1935 at Gaumont Studios, *The 39 Steps* is the clearest example of an earlier model for *North by Northwest*. Like Thornhill, Richard Hannay, the hero of this film, is falsely accused of a murder. Hannay is pursued by the police and is forced to resort to desperate actions as a means of escape. He attempts to expose the spy ring responsible for the murder, thereby establishing his innocence. Hannay's actions demonstrate the traits of a romantic action hero, but he is also forced into improvised acting, which he, like Thornhill, indulges in whilst maintaining a sense of humour. With the police in pursuit, Hannay boards a train to Scotland. As a means of hiding from the approaching police he dives into a railway carriage, embracing the woman who sits there alone. This stunt fails, however, since when the police return she hands him over. Later they are reunited and the woman finally accepts his story when she overhears one of the secret agents. In other words, the film produces twists and turns in a romantic relationship while pursuing the theme of an innocent man on the run, but the woman is not presented in the enigmatic style of Eve Kendall. As in *North by Northwest*,

film contexts

showy espionage movies

the story moves swiftly, with a journey structure pitching the hero into a variety of incongruous situations. *The 39 Steps* also involves a moment at which the hero appears to die from a gunshot but miraculously survives because of a hymn book that covered his heart.

Strangers on a Train, made in 1951 for Warner Brothers, also offers points of comparison with *North by Northwest*, with the theme of a persecuted innocent man. In *Strangers on a Train* the life of the main character, Guy Haines, a national tennis star, is thrown into disarray by a hoax which at first he interprets as ludicrous. A stranger, Bruno Anthony, suggests to Haines that they should exchange murders. Haines forgets about this conversation until he is made the chief suspect for the murder of his ex-wife. Anthony wishes to have his father murdered and demands that Haines fulfil their pact. Haines is forced to confront Anthony alone. Haines is isolated by the suspicion that he is responsible for the murder of his ex-wife. A strong atmosphere of suspense develops because Haines appears to be trapped, and the actions of Anthony are not evident to the police.

A contrast between *North by Northwest* and *Strangers on a Train* can be seen in the way that the former uses the context of a conflict involving national security, whereas the latter is concerned with the danger stemming from an individual who is deranged and driven by psychotic character traits. While Vandamm's motivation for trading in government secrets remains mysterious, Bruno Anthony is shown to be motivated by conflict with his father. Thus *Strangers on a Train* presents a much more psychological portrait of the villain, an obsessive stalker fixated on a national star as part of his criminal plans. Anthony's disturbed mind foreshadows the extended representation of a murderer's insanity in *Psycho*. *Strangers on a Train* develops a sense of horror in the scene that represents Anthony's murder of Haines's ex-wife. *North by Northwest*, in contrast, does not seek to make the audience dwell so much on the sadism of the villains. It is more like the showy espionage movies that developed subsequently in the James Bond cycle of films where the villain's evil is represented self-consciously as stereotypical.

A personal element enters the conflict between Vandamm and Thornhill because both characters are romantically involved with Eve. But this is not

film contexts

chaos invading everyday reality

developed to the point of absolute confrontation found in *Strangers on a Train* in which Haines struggles directly with Anthony, a character who has forcibly made himself Haines's alter ego. *North by Northwest* deliberately cultivates a different tone, which may be partly explained as a result of the different studio context. Warners, the studio behind *Strangers on a Train*, had a strong tradition in crime films, whereas MGM was known predominantly for glossy production values and musicals. While *Strangers on a Train* climaxes with a return to a fairground where the murder took place, *North by Northwest* builds to a climax in a new locale with connotations of American history and politics. Both films show chaos invading everyday reality through the actions of a criminal but in *North by Northwest* the final confrontation occurs in a space detached from everyday reality, providing a transition suitable to the adventure yarn.

In *Vertigo* the romantic narrative is more dominant. The story explores how Scottie, the James Stewart character, becomes romantically obsessed with a woman played by Kim Novak, initially known in the film as Madeline, whom he is supposed to be investigating on behalf of her husband Gavin Elster. In fact, Kim Novak plays a character, Judy, who has been employed by Elster to impersonate his wife. This creates a decoy, which helps Elster to conceal that what Scottie considers a suicide is in fact a murder.

In both *Vertigo* and *North by Northwest* the narrative centres on the experience of the main male character. In contrast to the emphasis on his actions, the female lead is presented as more mysterious. In both films the male character strives to understand what lies behind the woman's behaviour. In both cases appearances are presented as deceptive. In *Vertigo*, Scottie's relationship with the woman blurs the boundaries between investigation and romantic, emotional involvement. In the second half of the film Scottie's controlling behaviour leads to an exposé of her role as an accomplice in the murder of Elster's wife. The film, however, suggests that both the Kim Novak character and the James Stewart character are to an extent victims. Judy is used by the villain Gavin Elster in his plan to murder his wife, while Scottie suffers a mental breakdown after the apparent suicide has taken place. Although he is not

film contexts

elements from the thriller genre

accused of a crime, his failure to prevent the death brings back the problem of vertigo, established earlier in the narrative. This is compounded by mental degeneration, which appears to result from his feelings of guilt and failure. *Vertigo* presents a tragedy because the romantic feelings of the two main characters cannot succeed. They are both trapped by circumstance. The end of the film is abrupt and shocking, while the film as a whole has prompted extensive debate.

Vertigo offers parallels with *North by Northwest* in the representation of a romance that is transformed by elements from the thriller genre. Both films reveal the narrative truth behind mysterious developments in the plot before the ending. The scene in which the professor and his colleagues discuss why Thornhill has been abducted performs this function. In *Vertigo* we discover that the Kim Novak character was impersonating Madeline before this is revealed to Scottie. In both films these scenes reveal crucial information that eludes the main character and changes our relationship with the story. However, the scene of revelation in *Vertigo* has provoked more critical discussion because it suddenly introduces the viewpoint of the female character through a **flashback.** *North by Northwest* would, of course, be significantly changed through a sudden switch to Eve's perspective. This does occur at a minimal level with the shots that indicate her hidden feelings, and in a way the reconciliation between Eve and Thornhill interrupts suspense built up around the hero's lack of knowledge. Nevertheless the flashback in *Vertigo* has a more psychological impact, leaving the viewer potentially more aware of the woman's perspective.

The fact that *Vertigo* was less successful at the box office indicates the problems faced by Hollywood films that do not provide a happy ending. The greater psychological intensity of the relationship in *Vertigo*, with a slower pace in the narrative, may also have contributed to its relative box-office failure. Since *North by Northwest* was started before *Vertigo* it is very difficult to draw conclusions about how these projects may have affected one another. Hitchcock was clearly capable of moving quickly from one film to the next while consistently exploring themes and formal approaches that can be compared.

other cultural contexts

So far the main cultural reference points in this account of the film have been other films directed by Hitchcock and the style of Hollywood cinema. We have also mentioned the influence of different styles of film-making that emerged in the silent era, Soviet **montage** cinema and German expressionism. These distinctive styles had an impact on Hitchcock's development as a film-maker and to a certain extent influenced other film-makers in Britain and Hollywood. The montage style is vividly demonstrated by the work of Russian film-makers from the 1920s such as Sergei Eisenstein, but also more broadly has played a role in other cultural forms, including for example photomontage. Expressionism can be illustrated in the history of cinema by films such as *Nosferatu* (F.W. Murnau, 1922) or *Metropolis* (Fritz Lang, 1927). However, it is also a style evident in a wide range of cultural forms. Initially identified as a fine art movement in the early twentieth century, expressionism in cinema frequently emerged in the context of Gothic narratives conveying psychological unease.

Another wide-reaching art movement that emerged forcefully during the development of Hitchcock's career as a film-maker is surrealism. Surrealist film-makers such as Luis Buñuel sought to shock the audience with imagery that represented nightmare and dreamlike states of mind. At one level this surrealist film-making can be regarded as purely creative, with the film-maker seeking to break free from common sense or clichéd ideas of perception. At another level a surrealist film-maker like Buñuel thought that his work represented previously unacknowledged aspects of human experience.

Hitchcock never sought to develop the radical alternative to mainstream cinema that emerges in the three distinctive styles mentioned above. His devotion to crime thrillers helped to place his work within the mainstream of commercial cinema. However, it is useful to recognise points of comparison with styles outside mainstream popular cinema. Montage cinema foregrounded the dynamic properties of editing. Film-makers such as Eisenstein used juxtaposition between shots to convey political and

contexts — other cultural contexts

startling juxtaposition

historical themes. Hitchcock remains distant from such an overtly political approach, but his films include sections that clearly demonstrate the power editing has to evoke more general themes through startling juxtaposition.

In *North by Northwest* the prairie scene could be cited as an example for discussion about effects created through juxtaposition. In seeking an original format for the attack on the main protagonist, Hitchcock and Lehman move the film towards a more abstract form of expression. It is as if the encounter between innocence and evil has been stripped down to essential elements, the power of anonymously controlled technology against the unprotected human body. The emptiness of the landscape helps us to concentrate more on the purity of this juxtaposition between attacker and attacked, aeroplane and man. Although the scene does not present a political theme, the strong **cutting** back and forth may remind us of the approach adopted by the Russian film-makers of the montage school.

The influence of German expressionism is more evident in some other films directed by Hitchcock. However, certain readings of *North by Northwest* explore the psychological aspects of the story and also the way in which mise-en-scène contributes an uneasy mood related to psychological characterisation (for instance Rothman's analysis, summarised in Critical Responses, places some emphasis on the evocative, disturbing qualities of the mise-en-scène at key points in the narrative). It can also be argued that Hitchcock's films, including *North by Northwest*, draw extensively on the Gothic tradition of literature, which played a role in German expressionism. The idea of a double is used to a limited extent in *North by Northwest*, as mentioned previously (see Narrative & Form: Themes). In Gothic literature and German expressionism the appearance of a double haunting the main protagonist provided a stronger sense of psychological alienation. The figure of the mysterious Kaplan gestures towards this idea of the double.

Like the surrealists, Hitchcock was interested in shocking the audience, absurdity and the chilling effects achieved through strangeness. *North by Northwest* aims for maximum audience pleasure and consequently does not promote the disorientating effects of more experimental film-making.

other cultural contexts   contexts

ordinary existence to extraordinary circumstances

Nevertheless, the influence of a more absurdist viewpoint is apparent, such as when Vandamm uses Lester Townsend's house to disguise his true identity. The bizarre way in which the books in Townsend's study replace the drinks conveys the idea of incredible transformation, even though a logical explanation is provided in the form of Vandamm's machinations. The emphasis on accidental danger and the passage from ordinary existence to extraordinary circumstances is developed with an intensity that allows some comparison with the shock tactics of surrealism.

Clearly, creative comparison between the film and diverse cultural sources could be extended. The original novel of *The 39 Steps* by John Buchan and other relevant novels in the thriller genre may be considered as influences. The light-hearted and spectacular qualities in the James Bond films indicate how *North by Northwest* may have been an influence on work that followed.

critical responses

In *Hitchcock's Films*, Robin Wood provides an auteurist analysis of the film, drawing our attention to the relationship between *North by Northwest* and other films directed by Hitchcock. Wood places emphasis on the moral qualities of the story, suggesting that at the heart of the film is a concern with Thornhill's transformation. He changes from being a character who shows strong signs of cynicism and selfishness to become a hero who risks his life to defend Eve. We have already touched on this as one of the main themes in the story (see Narrative & Form: Themes, Narrative Structure and Characterisation). Wood's analysis, first published in the 1960s, is a key reference point in discussion of Hitchcock's artistic achievement.

Wood ends his chapter on *North by Northwest* enthusing: 'its charms, its deftness, the constant flow of invention, its humour and exhilaration are there for all to see' (Wood, 1989, p. 141). The aim of his analysis is to show that the film is 'a masterpiece' even though it is so 'relaxed'. He suggests that it is superior to *Goldfinger* (1964) primarily because *North by Northwest* is more serious, with the emphasis on Thornhill's transformation. Wood feels that with the opening, Hitchcock reached a high point of artistic expression

contexts — critical responses

'the precariousness of all human order'

in his exploration of instability beneath the surface of an apparently safe and controlled world. He writes:

> Hitchcock's sense of the precariousness of all human order has never been more beautifully expressed (though conveyed elsewhere – in *The Wrong Man* and *The Birds*, for instance – with greater intensity and overt seriousness) than in the mistake, due to sheer chance, by which Thornhill, going to send a telegram to his mother, finds himself kidnapped by gunmen.
> *Wood, 1989, p. 134*

Later in this discussion of the film Wood suggests that as the narrative develops we become increasingly sympathetic to Thornhill. By the final stages we are more likely to see the situation from Thornhill's perspective than from that of the professor. In this way Thornhill becomes identified with a clear moral purpose. Wood is keen to acknowledge the quality of lightness in the film. He argues that the moral subject matter does not overwhelm the comic style achieved through Hitchcock's direction.

Raymond Durgnat's analysis of the film can be found in *The Strange Case of Alfred Hitchcock*, published in 1974. For Durgnat *North by Northwest* is not amoral but remains remarkable for the way in which the ending 'depends on a great many non-moral factors and amoral decisions' (Durgnat, 1974, footnote p. 314). Durgnat contrasts the scale of the problems Thornhill is forced to confront with the triviality of his initial misdemeanours. He reflects on how the narrative leaves open the possibility for different moral reflections but refuses to dictate a strong message. He draws attention to the 'primitive' nature of Thornhill's request for help to Leonard at the end. Durgnat accepts that this provides a contrast with Thornhill's earlier dialogue, which contained so many 'wry' remarks. However, Durgnat indicates that it is typical of Hitchcock not to dwell on the transition to a more intense, social, moral issue.

Durgnat suggests that the meaning of the film's 'moral structure' is 'dramatic, or melodramatic and poetic' (Durgnat, 1974, p. 319). The inventiveness of the drama is illustrated, for example, by the drunken driving sequence in which a range of effects are brought together, including three

critical responses contexts

'perfectly happy' ending

different types of fear: '(1, fear of crashing off the cliff edge, 2, the only partly ethical fear of hitting and killing other road users, 3, fear of the following hoods)' (Durgnat, 1974, p. 320). Durgnat goes on to say that this sequence, which culminates with Thornhill crashing into a police car, illustrates Hitchcock's originality with a rapid combination and juxtaposition of different dramatic elements.

William Rothman's analysis of the film in *The 'I' of the Camera* (1988) concentrates on how the main characters are presented. He argues that the film refers back not only to *The 39 Steps*, but also to Hitchcock's British films of the 1920s. This comparison is illustrated by discussion of how the female protagonist is presented as trapped by a male-dominated world. However, *North by Northwest* is striking, as Rothman points out, for its 'perfectly happy' ending. His analysis involves an emphasis on transformation in the narrative alongside close attention to the style of film.

Rothman argues that *North by Northwest* displays Hitchcock's critical observations of American society. In the film America is a country 'where human beings and works of art alike are reduced to objects bought and sold' (Rothman, 1988, p. 175). The auction scene is an example of the way the film relates Eve's position to the alienation of being treated like a commodity. However, Rothman also suggests that Hitchcock's vision of America in *North by Northwest* is more benign, holding out for the possibility that the main characters can be saved and redeemed by love.

In discussing the Cary Grant role, Rothman concentrates at one point on the shot that shows Grant's face as he learns that Eve is a double agent. Rothman argues that this shot is extremely revealing of the character's conflicting emotions at this stage in the story. He also examines how we are made aware of Hitchcock's direction in relation to the presentation of Thornhill. It is argued that the light that falls on Thornhill's face from a nearby aeroplane provides a metaphor for 'the pain of enlightenment' experienced by the character at his realisation that Eve is a double agent (Rothman, 1988, p. 178). Rothman then goes on to say:

> Hitchcock's filming also suggests that Grant's pain is caused by being subjected to the camera's pitiless gaze. Hitchcock is responsible for Grant's anguish, which is a condition of his

contexts | **the audience**

> 'Eve's power to haunt and be haunted by the camera'
>
> enlightenment. Unless the author does whatever is in his power to secure Grant's happiness, Hitchcock will be exposed as inhuman.
>
> *Rothman, 1988, p. 178*

This interpretation is supported by the point that up to this stage in the narrative full information about Eve's role has been withheld from both Thornhill and the audience. Hitchcock must now orchestrate a redemptive climax or the story will become a cruel tragedy.

The analysis goes on to explore the presentation of Eve. Rothman draws attention to subtle aspects of style that may heighten our awareness of her predicament and her mystery. On more than one occasion she is framed by elements within the mise-en-scène which, according to Rothman, develops our awareness that she is reduced 'to the status of a commodity'. An example of this style of framing occurs when Eve first meets Thornhill on the train. At one point she is shown 'in profile within the frame of the closed compartment door' (Rothman, 1988, p. 181).

Later, Rothman considers the mise-en-scène of the scene when Eve meets Thornhill after the crop-dusting scene. He suggests that here the props and scenery, alongside 'repeated framings of Eve in profile or with her back to the camera' (Rothman, 1988, p.185) make the presentation more complex. These elements provide a sense that her real feelings are being suppressed as she tries to leave Thornhill. The mood of the sequence according to Rothman, 'declares Eve's power to haunt and be haunted by the camera' (Rothman, 1988, p. 186). Again the analysis appears to suggest that close attention to the direction intensifies our desire for the character to be saved and heightens our awareness of how the direction plays a personal, active role in the film's development.

the audience

Critical accounts of a film usually suggest, if only indirectly, how it may influence the audience. In practice, audience responses may vary a great deal. Critical analysis usually provides a specialised account of the film while actual audiences may be affected by different circumstances. These include the historical point at which the film is seen; whether it is viewed

the audience   contexts

audience responses vary

on video, television, DVD or in the cinema; whether you watch the film with a cinema audience, a group of friends, alone, or in the context of a course. Audience research might include an examination of whether variations in age, gender, class and race within the audience have an impact on reactions to a film such as *North by Northwest*. Audiences may be influenced by factors outside the film itself, including their own personal knowledge and experience of similar movies, ideas and opinion communicated by reviews, advertisements and publicity. Clearly response to the film may differ enormously between a young person who has not seen any films directed by Hitchcock or starring Cary Grant, and a Hitchcock fan who has seen *North by Northwest* several times before but is specifically interested in the details of film style used to deliver the narrative.

Approaches to analysis of media audiences have involved both quantitative and qualitative research. The former may provide statistical evidence about how audience responses vary according to a factor such as gender; qualitative research tends to be more open-ended, bringing together personal responses by different members of the audience. In the latter case an effort can be made by the researcher to ensure that the responses recorded are as free as possible rather than being framed by particular questions.

An issue that arises in film studies is whether audience research provides a challenge to approaches that concentrate on the film itself. As soon as we acknowledge the value of exploring how actual audiences respond, questions emerge about whether the specialised analysis of a critic or academic is still valid. Critical work, drawing on such areas of knowledge as psychoanalysis or even the study of narrative structure, involves ideas that may be detached from the vocabulary actual audiences use to discuss their experience of viewing a film. However, this does not invalidate the work of critical analysis. As we have seen, this can bring forward for debate arguments that are suggestive of different factors affecting the audience. A critic's specialised knowledge of the film and film history, as well as more general enquiries into human nature such as psychoanalysis, will provide points of contrast and comparison with our immediate response to a particular film such as *North by Northwest*.

contexts | **the audience**

many films offer a 'preferred' reading

Within film studies there are variations in the extent to which academic work reflects on how the audience may be affected by a film. Psychoanalytical approaches tend to suggest a level at which the film may affect us which is not immediately compatible with common-sense discussion of film viewing. There are differences between critics who use this approach. For instance, the issue of how passive the audience is in their response has provoked a range of theoretical arguments. Hitchcock's emphasis on leading the audience implies a submissive experience for the viewer but, as we have seen, it can be argued that a more active response occurs, even at a subliminal level, through possible identification with a leading character, the direction, or both in conjunction.

Another issue is whether our capacity to identify with the male character is significantly determined by our own gender; or whether this may be outweighed by, for example, empathy with this character's predicament as a human being. Analysis of *North by Northwest* suggests that the relationship between Thornhill and Eve involves playing up sexual differences. This means that an approach that considers the significance of gender in the film becomes more relevant. The film ultimately seeks to provide a unifying theme through heterosexual romance. However, the specialised analysis drawing our attention to how gender roles are presented indicates that the ending will affect us in different ways.

With the recognition that different audience responses are possible it is helpful to bear in mind that a film can be read in different ways. To read a film suggests some experience of particular conventions of narrative and film style. It has been argued that many films offer a 'preferred' reading. (This approach draws on a range of theoretical developments including the work of Stuart Hall. For instance, see 'Encoding/Decoding' in Hall et al. (eds), 1980.) This may involve the main ideas that the director and other creators behind the film seek to convey. The concept of a preferred reading also suggests that the message or meaning of the film may seem obvious due to other dominant ideas within society. The portrait of the villain in *North by Northwest*, for example, builds on our knowledge of archetypal villains developed within the crime genre and is possibly consolidated by fears of interference with national security developed during the Cold War.

the audience — contexts

> interpretation of films is a creative process

The character of Vandamm plays initially on our established ideas of morality, and then elaborates this sense of evil economically through reference to established ideas about how such a character might behave. At the same time he is not a realistic character so the film cultivates our enjoyment of the story as a fiction.

A 'counter reading' or 'oppositional' view of the text emerges when we highlight meanings within the film that are not immediately obvious or were clearly not intended by the film-makers. Since the film excludes explicit reference to political content a counter reading might emphasise how the film provides a communication that has an abstract quality. The reading could place more emphasis on tension between the film's entertainment qualities and the historical context in which it was made. Rothman's argument that the film involves a critical depiction of American society appears to be an example of a counter reading since this was not a perspective that early reviews drew attention to, and it is not obvious from writing by Hitchcock or Lehman that they intended this perspective.

The possibility of different readings reflects not only that audience responses are subjective, but also that interpretation of films is a creative process. A counter reading might convey pleasure in the film whilst resisting certain meanings which are central to the story. We may just enjoy certain moments of suspense without wishing to identify as fully with Thornhill as the ending appears to demand. We do not have to accept dominant ideas within the film, but instead our enjoyment or interest may involve a form of negotiation with the text (an argument developed by Christine Gledhill in 'Pleasurable Negotiations' in Pribram (ed.), 1988, and before this explained in, for example, Hall et al. (eds), 1980). Of course, the conditions of cinema – the darkness, the desire for fantasy, the special environment of a collective group – suggest that a less analytical approach will prevail, more in tune with Hitchcock's idea of film as a medium that envelops us with a dreamlike or nightmarish experience. But the possibility of different readings indicates how the audience response may be more varied, flexible and active. Ambiguity within the film can increase the range of responses.

bibliography

Altman – Nowell-Smith

general film

Altman, Rick, **Film Genre**, BFI, 1999
Detailed exploration of the concept of film genre

Bordwell, David, **Narration in the Fiction Film**, Routledge, 1985
A detailed study of narrative theory and structures

– – –, Staiger, Janet & Thompson, Kristin, **The Classical Hollywood Cinema: Film Style & Mode of Production to 1960**, Routledge, 1985; pbk 1995
An authoritative study of cinema as institution, it covers film style and production

– – – & Thompson, Kristin, **Film Art**, McGraw-Hill, 4th edn, 1993
An introduction to film aesthetics for the non-specialist; contains an analysis of *North by Northwest*, looking closely at narrative structure and narration

Branson, Gill & Stafford, Roy, **The Media Student's Book**, Routledge, 2nd edn, 1999

Buckland, Warren, **Teach Yourself Film Studies**, Hodder & Stoughton, 1988
Very accessible, it gives an overview of key areas in film studies

Cook, Pam & Bernink, Mieke (eds), **The Cinema Book**, BFI, 2nd edn, 1999

Corrigan, Tim, **A Short Guide To Writing About Film**, Harper Collins, 1994
What it says: a practical guide for students

Dyer, Richard with Paul McDonald, **Stars**, BFI, 2nd edn, 1998
A good introduction to the star system

Easthope, Antony, **Classical Film Theory**, Longman, 1993
A clear overview of writing about film theory

Hayward, Susan, **Key Concepts in Cinema Studies**, Routledge, 1996

Hill, John & Gibson, Pamela Church (eds), **The Oxford Guide to Film Studies**, Oxford University Press, 1998
Wide-ranging standard guide; includes a chapter by Barbara Creed that provides an overview of research and writing on film and psychoanalysis

Lapsley, Robert & Westlake, Michael, **Film Theory: An Introduction**, Manchester University Press, 1994

Maltby, Richard & Craven, Ian, **Hollywood Cinema**, Blackwell, 1995
A comprehensive work on the Hollywood industry and its products

Mulvey, Laura, 'Visual Pleasure and Narrative Cinema' (1974), in **Visual and Other Pleasures**, Indiana University Press, Bloomington, 1989
The classic analysis of 'the look' and 'the male gaze' in Hollywood cinema. Also available in numerous other edited collections

Nelmes, Jill (ed.), **Introduction to Film Studies**, Routledge, 2nd edn, 1999
Deals with several national cinemas and key concepts in film study

Nowell-Smith, Geoffrey (ed.), **The Oxford History of World Cinema**, Oxford University Press, 1996
Hugely detailed and wide-ranging with many features on 'stars'

general film bibliography

Thomson – Deutelbaum

Thomson, David, *A Biographical Dictionary of the Cinema*, Secker & Warburg, 1975
 Unashamedly driven by personal taste, but often stimulating

Truffaut, François, *Hitchcock*, Simon & Schuster, 1966, rev. edn, Touchstone, 1985
 Landmark extended interview

Turner, Graeme, *Film as Social Practice*, 3rd edn, Routledge, 1999
 Chapter four, 'Film Narrative', discusses structuralist theories of narrative

Wollen, Peter, *Signs and Meaning in the Cinema*, BFI, 1997, rev. edn,
 An important study in semiology

Readers should also explore the many relevant websites and journals. *Film Education* and *Sight and Sound* are standard reading.

Valuable websites include:

The Internet Movie Database at www.uk.imdb.com

Screensite at www.tcf.ua.edu/screensite/contents.html

The Media and Communications Site at the University of Aberystwyth at www.aber.ac.uk/~dgc/welcome.html

There are obviously many other university and studio websites which are worth exploring in relation to film studies

north by northwest

Aulier, Dan, *Hitchcock's Notebooks*, Bloomsbury Publishing, 1999

Bannon, Barbara, 'Double, Double, Toil and Trouble', *Literature and Film Quarterly*, vol. 13, no. 1, 1985

Biskind, Peter, *Seeing is Believing – How Hollywood Taught us to Stop Worrying and Love the Fifties*, Pluto Press, 1983

Braudy, Leo and Cohen, Marshall (eds), *Film Theory and Criticism – Introductory Readings*, 5th edn, Oxford University Press, 1985
 Contains Laura Mulvey's article 'Visual Pleasure and Narrative Cinema'

Brown, Royal S., *Overtones and Undertones*, University of California Press, 1994

Carroll, Noel, *Mystifying Movies – Fads and Fallacies in Contemporary Film Theory*, Columbia University Press, 1988

Cohan, Steven, 'Cary Grant in the Fifties; Indiscretions of the Bachelor's Masquerade', *Screen* vol. 33 no. 4, Winter 1992
 Cohan quotes from Richard Schickel, *Cary Grant, A Celebration*, Little Brown, Boston, 1983; Rothman (see below); and Stanley Cavell's article on *North by Northwest, Critical Inquiry*, vol. 7, no. 4, 1981, p. 769

Deutelbaum, Marshall and Poague, Leland (eds), *A Hitchcock Reader*, Iowa State University Press, 1986

bibliography — north by northwest

Drexel – Spoto

Drexel, John (ed.), *Facts on File Encyclopedia of the Twentieth Century*, Facts on File, New York, 1991

Durgnat, Raymond, *The Strange Case of Alfred Hitchcock*, Faber and Faber, 1974

Encarta 97 encyclopedia on CD-ROM

Engelhardt, Tom, *The End of Victory Culture – Cold War America and the Disillusioning of a Generation*, Basic Books, 1995
  Includes discussion of how secret service work developed in America during the 1950s

Finler, Joel, *Alfred Hitchcock – The Hollywood Years*, B.T. Batsford, 1992
  Includes information about box-office takings and production costs of Hitchcock's American films

Freedman, Jonathan and Millington, Richard (eds), *Hitchcock's America*, Oxford University Press, New York 1999
  This book contains an analysis by Richard Millington of *North by Northwest* which explains the 'pumpkin' reference and discusses the film in relation to McCarthyism amongst other arguments about the critical and progressive values of the film. The book also includes a chapter by Debra Fried, which discusses Hitchcock's use of the process shot

Gottlieb, Sidney (ed.), *Hitchcock on Hitchcock – Selected Writings and Interviews*, Faber and Faber, 1997

Gow, Gordon, *Hollywood in the Fifties*, A.S. Barnes and Co., New York; A Zwemmer Limited, London, 1971

Hall, Stuart et al. (eds), *Culture, Media, Language*, Hutchinson, 1980

Jeromski, Grace (ed.), *International Dictionary of Films and Filmmakers, volume 4, Writers and Production Artists*, St James Press, 3rd edn, 1997
  Includes entries on Ernest Lehman (by Philip Kemp), and Bernard Herrmann (by Joseph Milicia)

Katz, Ephraim, *The International Film Encyclopedia*, Macmillan Press Limited, 1980

Lehman, Ernest, *North by Northwest*, Faber and Faber, 1999

Modleski, Tania, *The Women Who Knew Too Much: Hitchcock and Feminist Theory*, Methuen, 1988

Naremore, James, *Acting in the Cinema*, University of California Press, 1988

Pribram, E. Deirdre (ed.), *Female Spectators – Looking at Film and Television*, Verso, 1988.
  Contains 'Pleasurable Negotiations' by Christine Gledhill

Rohmer, Eric and Chabrol, Claude, *Hitchcock: The First Forty Four Films*, Frederick Ungar Publishing Co., translation published in 1979

Rothman, William, *The 'I' of the Camera – Essays in Film Criticism, History and Aesthetics*, Cambridge University Press, 1988

Rubin, Martin, *Thrillers*, Cambridge University Press, 1999

Schatz, Thomas, *The Genius of the System – Hollywood Film-making in the Studio Era*, Faber and Faber, 1998; first published 1996

Smith, Susan, *Hitchcock: Suspense, Humour, Tone*, BFI, 2000

Spoto, Donald, *The Dark Side of Genius – The Life of Alfred Hitchcock*, Plexus, 1994

north by northwest bibliography

Spoto – Wood

Spoto, Donald, *The Art of Alfred Hitchcock*, Anchor Books, 1997

Unterburger, Amy L. (ed.), *International Dictionary of Films and Filmmakers, volume 3, Actors and Actresses*, 3rd edn, St James Press, 1997
  Includes an entry on Eva Marie Saint (by Stuart M. Kaminsky, updated by David E. Salamie)

Wood, Robin, *Hitchcock's Films Revisited*, Columbia University Press, 1989
  This contains Wood's study of Hitchcock films, first published in 1965, with a reconsideration of the films and Wood's theoretical approach after two decades of teaching film studies. The analysis of *North by Northwest* referred to in this Note was written for the original book in 1965

cinematic terms

auteur – picaresque

auteur the director, when priority is given to his/her influence on the film through critically acclaimed originality of style and/or original development of distinctive themes

classical Hollywood from approximately 1917 to 1960, due to a consistent style with a clearly defined approach to film form, Hollywood cinema has been described as classical Hollywood

closure a term used to describe the tendency of narrative films to conclude without ambiguity. The aim of such endings is to provide a satisfying and coherent resolution of developments introduced in the narrative

continuity editing describes an approach to editing that emphasises how actions, events and spaces in the film are connected in a plausible, coherent fashion. Continuity editing usually minimises digression and distraction, putting the focus on smooth development of fictional or non-fictional patterns, using typical editing conventions such as shot/reverse shot, point of view shots, establishing shots, and, much more infrequently, match on action editing

cutting describes the effect of ending individual shots through editing without the use of fade, wipe, or dissolve

dissolve a gradual transition from one shot to the next involving momentary superimposition of images

equilibrium a period in the narrative that presents stability and freedom from conflict and disruptive events. The concept was used by Todorov in narrative analysis

flashback a section of the film that presents a period of time prior to that at which the narrative began or an earlier point in the narrative shown from a new perspective

genre a category used to classify different types of story, drawing attention to the relationship between various works. Genres may be distinguished by a range of factors including subject matter, style, marketing and effect on the audience

high angle shot in this kind of shot the camera looks down on the action. This may convey a character's state of vulnerability

identification when the viewer shares the viewpoint and perspective of a character in the film. Also used to describe the process whereby the viewer shares the viewpoint of the film as a whole

low angle shot in this kind of shot the camera's low position may convey a sense of disorientation, detachment, and/or make characters and objects more dominating

low-key lighting a style of lighting that involves strong contrasts between shadow and light

match on action when a cut involves a transition from one perspective on an action to another perspective as the same action develops. Thus a match on action preserves continuity but also provides a variation in the style of editing

montage an approach to editing developed by Russian film-makers after the Revolution. It involves an emphasis on radical juxtaposition of diverse shots as a means of presenting political and historical conflict

picaresque a story in which a hero or rogue goes through a series of episodic adventures

cinematic terms

point of view shot – traits

point of view shot a shot that provides the visual perspective of a character looking within the world of the story

realism a style that seeks to convince the viewer that the film is true to life. In a fiction film this may be conveyed through pertinent themes and the way the film has been constructed, for example through the use of real locations or non-actors. There is debate about whether different approaches are 'realistic' and if 'realism' is possible

rear projection this technique may also be described by the term 'process shot'. It involves a shot that is taken in front of film which has been shot earlier and projected through a transparent screen

scene a section of the film occurring in one location, and over a distinct period of time, which is not interrupted by cuts to action occurring in other locations or during a different period of time

screenplay this includes dialogue and also the narrative structure and screen directions provided by the scriptwriter

sequence a distinct section of the film, involving more than one scene, but united through concentration on a specific aspect of the narrative

shot/reverse shot an editing pattern that involves cutting back and forth, usually between two characters communicating

superimposition this describes the effect of images overlaid on the film

themes the main ideas that the film narrative conveys. A theme can be an idea that is developed by different parts of the narrative, or ideas that are given great significance at a specific point in the story as an explanation of narrative events

traits aspects that define a character's personality and motivation, which emerge clearly through the action and dialogue

credits

production company
Metro-Goldwyn-Mayer

director
Alred Hitchcock

associate producer
Herbert Coleman

screenplay
Ernest Lehman

photography
Robert Burks

editor
George Tomasini

art director
Robert Boyle

special effects
A. Gillespie

music
Bernard Herrmann

titles
Saul Bass

cast
Roger O. Thornhill – Cary Grant
Eve Kendall – Eva Marie Saint
Phillip Vandamm – James Mason
Mrs Clara Thornhill – Jessie Royce Landis
professor – Leo G. Carroll
Lester Townsend – Philip Ober
Leonard – Martin Landau
'Mrs Townsend' – Josephine Hutchinson
Valerian – Adam Williams